Twisdom

A Philosopher Ponders Life
In 140 Characters or Less

TomVMorris

A Wisdom/Works Book
MorrisInstitute.com

Twisdom™

A Wisdom/Works Book

This first on demand edition is made available
at internet-speed in 2009.
For more copies, visit MorrisInstitute.com,
Twisdom.me, or MoreTwisdom.com.
It's also available on Amazon.com
and at any traditional bookseller
with a good sense of humor
and a solid grasp of history.

Designed by Dennis Walsak and ModularGraphics.

"I give it about a month before someone publishes a best seller consisting of nothing but their tweets – you maybe?"

Peter de Jager / @pdejager
About a month ago....

Contents

.

6

The Great Gift of Twitter Wisdom
A Foreword by Mariel Hemingway

I didn't know Tom Morris until I came to know Twitter. I think we joined approximately the same time. We met through one of his random "tweets" that just couldn't be ignored. I was busy doing my thing – a bit of admittedly shameless self-promotion for my then upcoming cookbook and developing brand, while also genuinely wanting to offer a few words of guidance or kindness to the growing Twitter followers I was drawing in. It has been an interesting process of finding out how you can relate to other people within the limits of 140 characters.

Then Tom arrived and spoke of things that were like breaths of air on the network. I was trying to find my voice, while Tom seemed to already know what to say, mainly because he just said whatever he had on his mind or heart that day. He spoke of absolutely anything that came up, and if nothing came up, he brought up the most interesting point of view on issues of the self.

Tom is affecting people on Twitter, but not in the way that most others do. He is different. He does not shove book promo pages or websites down your throat on a constant basis. He offers his musings on love, freedom, security, remembrance, death, and service. He pulls apart his feelings on connection and oneness and how real happiness comes about in a life. He is a unique voice on Twitter and in my life. When I see him online, I smile, knowing that the interaction or conversation is going to go deeper and become more interesting than it has been in the past several minutes, or hours, if he has been away.

Tom Morris makes us think about the world differently, and the things we take for granted. He helps us understand in a way that invokes a sense of ease in who we are. Tom's voice is beyond prolific – he is spontaneous and inspired with each word he submits to the world. He is a gift to have as a friend and a gift to this crazy social network we call the "Twitterverse." His important point of view reminds us that we can bring more humanity and consciousness into our lives, and therefore shift into a greater awareness.

Even when we're overindulging in computer communication that could be mindless, Tom makes it feel useful, and makes us feel better for having been here. Thank you, Tom, for creating a new form of sacred space within which we can grow and learn in the ether.

The World According to Twisdom
A Foreword by Kathy Ireland

If twitter.com is the world's biggest and greatest new party, our miraculous mix master is surely TomVMorris. We have never looked in each other's eyes, and yet our friendship forged on Twitter is one of the most powerful connections in my life. Our families know and love each other in bursts of 140-character micro-blogging. Just five years ago, I would have thought such closeness was impossible online. But that would have been just silly, backward thinking. New things are happening with Twitter.

Tom's values, ethics, wisdom, and years of commitment to Truth, Beauty, Goodness and Unity are the foundations we all need to triumph in this new age of information intimacy overload. Knowledge is power, and a proper use of power calls for wisdom. Without a foundation of ethical understanding, knowledge can be put to use in cruel and damaging ways. We all seek to be well informed, thoughtful, and wise. Tom's twisdom gives us the ability to be the authors of our dreams with smart, humorous truth and great beauty. From now on, after the appearance of this wonderful book of treasures, the greatest Twitter wisdom will be better known as twisdom. A new word has entered our lexicon. It conveys the ability to be wise, warm, and true in brief and helpful statements about life.

I first became aware of Tom when I read his great book, If Aristotle Ran General Motors. If you haven't read it, please buy it today. It will protect your heart and your finances! Had GM's leaders acted in the manner prescribed by our Dr. Tom, their bankruptcy could surely have been avoided. Tom wants us to use twisdom to find safe harbors in our voyages. We can do great things in our lives, but only if we're guided and protected by the right values. In a world of unexpected storms, we need twisdom for the journey!

Solid deposits of insight are in these pages, and you can make the ideal wisdom withdrawal for help in dealing with any situation. Frightened? Anxious? Angry? Joyous? No problem, Tom's brilliant wit becomes your own. You need never worry about crossing a line from healthy to harmful, if you follow the guidelines here. This book of Twisdom is the essential resource and philosophical guide for navigating a brave new way of communicating that can change your life, as it has mine. It's also a great deal of fun!

Here's to twisdom! May it bring you the illumination, peace, and joy that those of us who follow our Wisdom Mentor, TomVMorris, are blessed with every day on twitter.com.

Introduction
From a Philosopher as Surprised as You

Twitter is the world's greatest cocktail party, and no one has to clean up afterwards, or even pay the tab. It's the new electronic campfire we now sit around to talk and laugh and even sing. It's an endless conversation like no other, and it's just starting to pick up steam.

It's also the new water cooler for the creative class – the social break room for people who don't work in an office. And for those who do, it's the ultimate instant coffee break. With thirty seconds or three minutes of total immersion, or more, you can be socializing with people all over the country, and around the globe, sharing quick tales of weal and woe that range from the mundane all the way to the metaphysical. There is instant advice, encouragement, and information to be had any time you stick your toes into the Twitter stream – if you've found a good spot on the bank of this wild new river to perch.

I've been using and enjoying this novel social medium and "micro-blog" website under the carefully devised codename, TomVMorris, for about eight weeks now. To my tremendous surprise, it's a distinctive and amazing experience.

What Twitter Really Is

Twitter is not mainly about telling the world, or your fourteen followers, what you had for lunch. And it's not just about Ashton and Oprah, or who can collect the most followers the quickest. It's about building a new form of community. It's about learning. It's about support, inspiration, and daily motivation. And it's also about fun. But the most important aspect of Twitter for me is that, if you do things right, you surround yourself with an incredible collection of people from around the world who are eager to share their best questions and insights about life. They're all looking for new wisdom and hope.

There is communal thinking on Twitter at a level and in a form I've never seen before. Almost every day, and often many times a day, a topic comes up that causes me, as a practical philosopher and as simply a curious individual, to ponder a bit, and then share the results of that pondering in the 140 character increments, or "tweets" that Twitter allows. One comment will spark another, and before long, people of different ages and walks of life are engaged in an extended conversation of brief bursts that add up to new realizations for everyone involved. I've gone from two followers to several thousand in my first eight weeks of tweeting. This means that, when I send a tweet, that many people in principle could read it. And if they like it, they can retweet it, or copy and tweet it on to their circles of followers, many of whom might then, if they also resonate with what I've said, send it on again, and then maybe even become my followers as well. In turn, seeing their use of my own little thought, I may join their circle. It's literally unimaginable these days how far a single tweet can go in its effort to do a little good in the world. The new connectivity based around Twitter is immensely and surprisingly powerful.

The New Media and Our Need for Wisdom

One day, someone in my Twitter stream mentioned Susan Boyle, the old fashioned lady who made such a stir worldwide in the Spring of 2009 with her appearance on the television show Britain's Got Talent. The YouTube video of her performance was like a shot fired round the world, and within days it had been viewed many millions of times. People of nearly all ages, races, and occupations had tears in their eyes as they watched this simple forty seven year old lass from a small village in Scotland undergo an powerful instant metamorphosis from the apparently dowdy, hopeless, and even derided misfit we first saw on stage into a source of deeply moving vocal beauty and spiritual uplift.

In a matter of seconds, the live audience on the video, many of whom had just been laughing at this unlikely contestant for stardom and shaking their heads in disbelief during her short interview onstage, all began shouting acclaim and rising to their feet as she finally burst into song. At that moment in all the replays, viewers by the millions watching on the web began having emotional reactions of their own, and within minutes were posting the video on their personal blogs, or linking to it and talking about it on social media sites like Face Book and Twitter.

It was on Twitter that I first learned of this video, and clicked a link that allowed me to watch it. Like everyone else, I was stunned by how a woman whose appearance was so out of step with our modern culture of celebrity beauty and fashion could just be herself unapologetically and boldly, in the most public way imaginable, and move us all to our depths. Within minutes of seeing her performance, many viewers were even questioning their values, reassessing their unspoken and often unconscious prejudices about appearance and importance, and even examining themselves for that inner spark of courage that Susan Boyle most obviously enjoyed.

As I reflected on what I had seen of Susan on that occasion and considered her immediate lessons for the rest of us, I typed and tweeted. Instantly, people started retweeting my thoughts, passing along those short reflections to others. As I saw what ideas touched people the most, I continued to think and tweet. And as I witnessed an unexpected explosion of interest in these thoughts, I spontaneously decided that I'd do a special blog that day on The Huffington Post, where I recently began philosophizing weekly, simply to share those tweets, or twitter reflections, and to provide an example of the unlikely musing that is now flashing around the internet. So I wrote up a quick blog that afternoon on my recent use of Twitter as a place for personal and communal thinking, and I used as my illustration the Twitter event Susan's video had unleashed.

The tweets I originally sent and then reblogged on HuffPo were all simple observations that I had sent out a few seconds or a few minutes apart. My intent was that if they stimulated the further thoughts of others, they would have done their proper work. To give a sense of how this unfolded, and of what often transpires on Twitter in my experience, I'll simply reproduce a few below, in the order they were sent.

It's always an interesting challenge to offer a new perspective, or a little illumination on something in life, in the standard 140-character Twitter format. In this case, I surmised the usefulness of a topic announcement with each connected offering, since each has to stand on its own and not get lost in the fast moving stream of constantly changing tweets from computers, laptops, blackberries, and i-phones. I'd sit and contemplate the topic, tweet, then think a minute more and tweet again. I'd also look to see which of my prior tweets were generating responses. There was much more of a reaction to each of them that day than I ever would have guessed.

Meanwhile, in the twitter stream of my followers' electronic screens, dozens or hundreds of new tweets from other people may have intervened between any two of mine. So I put Susan's name at the head of each new tweet, as you'll see. If you haven't ever viewed the remarkable video that launched all this, and so much more, then you might want to immediately Google "Susan Boyle on Britain's Got Talent," stop reading this, and go watch right the original video, her first appearance on the show, right now. Then, you can have a full perspective on the simple tweets I sent that day, and what happened with them as a result. Here are just three of the many that are reproduced later in this book, to give you a flavor for how they played out.

Susan Boyle: The picture of courage, immense self-possession, perfect centeredness, inner beauty, and a spirit of fun.

Susan Boyle: One small person amazing, inspiring, and energizing the world.

Susan Boyle: The Imponderable, Improbable, even Impossible Dream empowering us all to reach and achieve.

It was quite an experience, seeing the new media of YouTube, Twitter, and the Huffington Post all come together in mutually reinforcing ways, to bring people instant images of something new, and to make possible shared reflections on what we were feeling as a result of the experience. And all this happened in a way, and at a speed, that could not have been imagined just a few years ago.

Of course, several weeks later, we all saw a very different side of the Susan Boyle story, and I've tweeted further on the lessons we can learn from that. The internet cauldron of immediacy created a media frenzy surrounding this previously private lady, and brought immense pressures into her life unlike anything she had ever felt. She was swept up into instant fame, career promises, critical scrutiny, and personal stress to an extent that she never could have anticipated. And in the final voting on the television show that had launched her into international notoriety, she came in a surprising second place for the overall competition. Then she promptly suffered a widely publicized emotional and psychological breakdown from it all.

In an age of new, immediate media, wonderful and terrible things are possible. We need perhaps more wisdom than ever to deal with it all, and to make of the possibilities available something good. That's one thing Twitter has been able to provide in a novel way – a social space where new wisdom can develop through real-time interaction among people all over the world, and older insights about life can be propagated to those who need them, ideas and perspectives that are relevant to what we're now seeing, hearing, and living. The new media help create a world that requires new wisdom, and fortunately they also provide new ways for that wisdom to arise.

Twitter Is What You Make It

While some younger friends were originally urging me to try Twitter, other friends were warning me off it. And I now understand both perspectives. As an experiment, I once clicked on the universal Twitter stream named "Everyone" that was available for a while on the basic Twitter web page, as it was displayed on my monitor. This immersed me in the main current of Tweets from all over the world. I refreshed the page every four seconds, scanning and reading everything I could as fast as I was able, and I did this for a stretch of ten minutes – an eternity in Central TwitterTime.

I didn't see any quotations from great thinkers. There were no interesting musings on life. There didn't seem to be much real social interaction at all, with people directing remarks or responses to other individuals. There were just lots of soliloquies on what people were doing, however trivial. There was some profane language. There was complaining and venting. But there was almost nothing like what I see in my own Twitter village every time I open up the screen.

I was reminded that, like almost everything else in our world, Twitter is what we make of it. I've found people who want to use it to think, touch lives, work together, support each other, and meet other like-minded individuals wanting the same. It's an amazing circle of novelists, cartoonists, comic book writers and illustrators, editors, consultants, corporate and personal coaches, journalists, executives, marketers, moms and dads, and various celebrities who are real people with strong interests in ideas, and in being helpful with their time. It's a great retreat! It's a tremendous advance! It's an idea camp for us all! It's a self-selected collection of vibrant and generous personalities, the likes of which

I've never seen thinking and playing together.

I wanted to share a slice of that experience here. But I could not begin to represent the full give and take of ideas, the flow of conversations, the jokes and puns and other funny things that spontaneously appear on the screen. And since that is the heart of my experience of Twitter, I don't pretend for a moment to be presenting in this little book a representative slice of this social phenomenon. I'm just offering some of my own tweets that have touched people, or sparked conversations, elicited hearty agreement, and apparently made the rounds far beyond my tight circle of great followers, and those I follow as well. I present here a representative sample of the tweets I've done that stand more or less on their own, outside of their original context, and perhaps convey some insight, or Twitter wisdom, about a few of the things we all confront in our lives.

Twisdom: Twitter Wisdom

In the short bursts of thought and commentary that Twitter allows, we can all turn into aphorists. Critics could dismiss what results as nothing more than fortune cookie wisdom, without the cookie. But the nuggets of insight that Twitter allows can in principle be much more than that. Like almost anything else, it's up to us.

Twitter exchanges won't typically replicate a Yale philosophy seminar, or a colloquium at Notre Dame. It's a place not for abstruse theory but for practical insight. I'm offering in this book those tweets of mine from my short time of experiencing Twitter that have been most appreciated by others, and that represent one philosopher's use of this discipline of succinctness and sociability to help clarify some of the small confusions and needs in our lives. As Steven Johnson recently said in a Time Magazine cover story on this whole phenomenon, "Twitter turns out to have surprising depth." One tweet can change your life, or on a much smaller scale, make your day. I hope some of the musings collected here will serve a positive function for you, in your own contemplation of the wonder and mystery of your life.

I don't pretend to profundity here. Wisdom is often more down to earth and humble than that. It's frequently just a reminder of something we know and need to live. Or it's a slightly new angle on an old realization. It's a matter of perspective. Or it's a call to action, and an inspiration to go take some initiative right away.

I have named this book of Twitter wisdom, and collectively, these tweets, with a new term I've coined – Twisdom – because I believe that these insights have originated in a new way, out of the novel space and collective thinking that can occur on Twitter, in short bursts, and on the run. But that's the way we do most things these days – in short bursts, and on the run. So perhaps the twisdom that has come about in the same way may be well suited to the situations we confront, and the insights we need, at precisely this moment in time.

I hope that, if this book gives you a flavor of what you'd like to experience each day, you'll decide to join me and my other new friends on Twitter and share some twisdom of your own. Follow me, TomVMorris, and I'll look forward to joining you as well in this new and exciting exploration of ideas and possibilities together.

Twisdom

Week One
First Thoughts – Getting our Tweet Wet
And Learning the Rules

Let the tweeting begin!

The morning: Right after the fog, clarity comes.

Before engagements, prior to the mix, a brief, full moment of calm.

Bird songs begin the soundtrack for this docu-drama of life. A distant rustle. A buzzing bee.

The morning: This morning, never to be again. Attend to it. Relish it. Use it well.

A crunch of toast, a spread of jam, a topping of nuts, and I just am.

"Everything on earth is subject to change." The I Ching

Lemons to lemonade: When the place burned down where the band Deep Purple was about to record, they wrote the hit "Smoke on the Water."

"The loftiest towers rise from the ground." - Chinese proverb. We all start from where we are.

Just wrote on our economic and political crises, "Living in Plato's Cave." Plato and Aristotle nailed it for us.

A thought: One half of human nature got us into our current troubles. It will take the other half to get us out.

I'm reading Cicero's classic essay on old age – the great Levenger edition, "On a Life Well Spent." (Levenger.com)

Pondering: Just a prelude to contemplating. Hoping to have some time left for realizing – or, at least, concluding.

Watching Entertainment Tonight. Philosophers have to keep up.

 "Life is an irreversible process and for that reason its future can never be a repetition of the past." - Walter Lippmann

Just started Twitter. So far, I could share with more people by standing in the back yard and talking loud. Appreciate you who listen!

Small seeds can create a forest.

From Cicero: If right before death, you were given the chance to start this life all over again, from infancy, would you?

Start to a philosopher's day: First waking thought – I wonder what happens if you microwave dog food?

"Philosophy begins in wonder." - Aristotle

Rereading Cicero today on old age. His mouthpiece, Cato, says the best preparation for it is a life well spent in learning and doing nobly.

Human nature story of the day: "Man dies of Viagra overdose." No, not Hef – a 28 yr old on his last quest. Universal wisdom: moderation.

"The market wants truth." I've urged Truth, Beauty, Goodness, and Unity for years. Without Truth, things get ugly, bad, and broken.

We're all living in Plato's Cave, and the market is the low level of the cavern. The way out: Courage to give up illusions and face truth.

A thought for the day: "All life is experiment. The more experiments you make, the better." - Emerson

In business as well as politics, when gamesmanship prevails over common sense, we all lose. What a way to start a century!

Wisely, god buries in night and darkness what will result from days to come, and laughs if men are more afraid than need be. - Horace

Keep this in mind: be calm, and put in order the things at hand; all else is carried as if by a river. - Horace, Ode III 29.

I've been told to be careful on Twitter – philosophy may go viral. I do remember itching quite badly when I first read Hegel. But no worry.

If Socrates Tweeted: Know You! The unexamined life – No Way! Wise? Who, me?

Socrates: The originator of the Hemlock Maneuver. Don't try this at home.

Be wise, be happy; be unwise, be otherwise.

If Descartes had been on Twitter, he might have expressed its impetus for all of us: "I think, therefore I tweet. I tweet, therefore I am."

I ponder the Twitter question, "What are you doing?" What, indeed, am I doing?

"To master yourself is the greatest mastery." - Seneca

Seneca's wisdom test: "The wise man is joyful, happy, and calm, unshaken; he lives on a plane with the gods." It's a great ideal.

A nice reminder in the face of trouble – Dr. Johnson to Boswell: "Consider, Sir, how insignificant this will appear a twelvemonth hence."

Tweeting: A new form of diversion within Plato's Cave, or possibly some breadcrumbs to follow to find our way out? As usual, it's up to us.

"Two quite opposite qualities equally bias the mind – habits and novelty." - Jean de la Bruyere (1645-1696)

"A situation becomes favorable only when we adapt to it." - I Ching

"Man has unrivalled powers of self-adaptation." - Charles Kingsley

It's a beautiful morning with incredible light: Signs of spring. The weekend will be in the 70s. It's beach walk time. Come on down!

Most-Famous-Philosopher-at-the-Beach Award goes to Epictetus. Freed slave. Philosopher of liberation. Great Stoic. Fun and funny.

"There is no mendacity more unscrupulous than that which sets out to calumniate those whom its utterers choose to deem the enemies of God."

That's from a 1902 book on Shakespeare and Voltaire. Isn't it amazing how our use of language has changed? Still: a treat as a tweet.

When I once started doing things on TV, I realized my face was better for radio. I know now that my entire body is perfect for Twitter.

This whole tweet was done with my nose.

A positive philosophy for everyday life doesn't have to consist of empty, superficial hyperbole. The real truth is exciting enough.

Tweeted this with my elbow.

Just came across a great phrase in Tocqueville's Democracy in America, 'the art of being free.' Pondering that one a bit.

While Plato was wrong to think that knowledge guarantees goodness, a deeper understanding of human nature does tend to affect our behavior.

I'm reading about executives being more Ayn Rand-y than ever. There's a lot of new interest in self-interest.

You do wonder sometimes: If every speck of self-interest were to vanish from the earth, would everything just stop and everyone go mute?

What the world needs is enlightened self-interest that works for the greater good of all.

Accountability tends to exist more in relationships characterized by proximity (face2face), longevity, and density (mutual friends, etc).

Aristotle believed a city should only be so big, to function well, and you can have only a few real friends. What would he make of Twitter?

Just drank a smoothie way too fast and had a major head freeze! Not good for any thinker! How does that happen? Got to thaw the neurons.

The best leaders are great teachers. They educate, inspire, and guide. And they're often too busy to read books on: leadership.

Most of the best books on leadership aren't addressed to most of the best leaders, but to those who aspire to that role, and to do it well.

Top leaders often tell me that they tend to read history, science, politics, fiction, and – here's where I get lucky – philosophy.

If, as a writer, you can combine two or more of those genres, you've hit the jackpot for potential impact.

There are so many authors on Twitter. They're rather tweet than work!

We're all looking for Twitter to play a major role in up-coming novels – as long as it doesn't prevent the writing of those novels.

Always remember one of the most common pieces of ancient wisdom ever: We become like the people we're around. That includes Twitter.

Tweeted with my nose today and with an elbow. Was going to use a toe but there were 10 possible, and it got complex. Exploring social media.

For those who joined me today: Don't worry, I'm not crazy – Just fascinated at the newness/convenience/almost anything goes nature of this.

As the stock market fell again, I noticed people's faces all around me all day. Everyone looked normal. And that said all the right things.

Gotta go watch another guilty pleasure: Choosing between Idol and Millionaire Matchmaker – if Kant had lived now!

"A human being is never what he is but the self he seeks."
- Octavio Paz. Good morning twitterers. I'm on late due to early meetings.

Got to get my philosophical mojo going, and up to speed fast. Hey: If a tree falls in the forest and there's no one there to tweet it ...

"In general, the goodness of non-spiritual assets depends on our spiritual character, and the goodness of that, on wisdom." - Socrates (Meno)

Thought for the day: Is Twitter your catharsis, or is Twitter your muse?

Reading a book that nobody seems to know, yet was a huge influence long ago. You have to get off the beaten path for novel insights.

If you read what everyone else is reading, you'll think what everyone else is thinking.

The web-use paradox: You have to get enough information to stimulate your own creativity, but not so much as to shut it down.

So many seem to scramble and scheme to get more "followers" here. But what's important is who they are and what they do with your tweets.

Tom's TwitRule #1: Follow Twitwits and never nitwits, and the same will find you as well.

Tom's TwitRule #2: Birds of a feather tweet together.

Tom's TwitRule #3: Tweet others as you would want to be tweeted.

Tom's TwitRule #4: Never assume that Twitter-reality is a fair sample class of outer-reality.

Tom's TwitRule #5: What happens in Twitter, stays in Twitter – unless you take it out and use it.

Tom's TwitRule #6: Twitter is not what you want it to be; it is what you make it.

Tom's TwitRule #7: An interesting or useful tweet has feet – once you send it out, it can go quite far.

Tom's TwitRule #8: Whether your Twitter goal is to give or to get, or to blend the two, will become clear within a few tweets.

Tom's TwitRule #9: For those who just know you here, you are what you tweet. For those who know you elsewhere, you tweet what you are.

Tom's TwitRule #10: Less is more, more or less.

Tom's TwitRule #11: If we don't get away from our screens now and then, we have little to bring to our screens when we're here.

Tom's TwitRule #12: When you have to start getting food delivered so that you can keep up with your tweeps, you just might be a TwitterHead.

Tom's TwitRule #13: When you find yourself talking to family members aloud in 140 character increments, you just might be a Twitterhead.

Tom's TwitRule #14: If you chatter on about how many followers you have, and aren't a cult leader, you're clearly a Twitterhead.

Tom's TwitRule #15: If you find yourself seriously torn between enjoying a beautiful day and sitting inside to tweet, you may have a problem.

Enough for now! And that's a word we don't hear ... enough.

We all have an emotion telescope. When trouble comes, don't peer through the end that makes it look bigger. Flip it and change your view.

One of life's top imperatives is this: Encourage quality wherever you can.

What do you do when you first lose a follower here? Grieve? Panic? Wonder? Do you retreat from the very last tweet? Second-guess yourself?

Do you assume that they hit the "Don't Follow This Nut" button by accident?

And of course, you can't call them back – they're not following you any more. What to do? It's a true perplexity: The defeat of the tweet.

Watching E! News. Plato and Aristotle are looking down at me with frowns ... Wait! They just want me to turn up the sound!

I'm 2-followers away from 100. As if it matters, but still, tell your friends. Support your local sage. After a week, a crowd!

Self-sabotage is the #1 cause of failure in our culture.

I have a very nasal voice that makes me cringe; yet, I've been a public speaker for 20 years. Passion, fun, and ideas do it!

Every downturn goes away. The pendulum swings. A massive amount of what's going on now is emotional.

The key to life is the same as the key to Twitter: Edit, simplify, learn, rethink, and "Update."

We need to align our unconscious attitudes with our highest aspirations. No divided minds!

Coffee and sunshine are now snowplowing my neural pathways for the traffic of a new day. May we all have a taste of synaptic glory!

Coffee black and dense and oiled, one more cup and my brain is roiled!

Coffee Cup 2.5 – right here. Engineered specially for social media. Chock Full o' Nuts!

Breakfast with the birds: Male and female cardinals a few feet away, having a great meal. They seem not to be concerned about the economy.

"Goodness is the only investment that never fails." - Thoreau.

Writing helps me think. Tweeting helps me think succinctly.

In a short time here, you can spot the communitarians and

solipsists, the hawkers, gawkers, and all the great talkers. A multitude tweets!

In old-fashioned terms, when what you do is a mission first, and a business second, it has real heart and a special power.

The Beautiful Day Conundrum: To tweet or not to tweet, that is the question ... Maybe 'tis nobler for the mind to get some fresh air and sun.

Plato believed we each need a vivid vision of The Good to guide us and motivate us in life. Otherwise, we get lost in distractions.

Someone asked a very original question just now: Is there a connection between fear of death and brand loyalty?

Possibly: In fear of ultimately losing all, we cling tight to what we love. Brand is a band to tie us to earth.

I think spirituality can also lead to brand loyalty: When you see love and quality in a brand, your nobler self attaches to it.

A friend likes to say that your brand is the sum total of promises you make and keep to everyone touched by what you do. Nice perspective.

The Sun was Plato's model of The Good. When it's in our life, we see everything in its light. Going out for some Good, now.

A leadership challenge can be like playing 3 D chess with living, thinking pieces who are also playing their own similar 3 D chess, etc.

But in this game, you can't just move pieces, but must convince them that it is good, or at least in their interest, to move ... there.

Nice reminder from Hamlet: "Use every man after his desert, and who shall 'scape whipping? Use them after your own honor and dignity."

In other words, don't do unto others as they deserve, but as you, in your highest heart of hearts, deserve to do.

Another famous spin: "Treat others as if they were what they ought to be, and you help them to become what they are capable of being."

In a sea of sameness, celebrate excellence. You get more of it that way.

Things just pop into my head and now I have some place to put them – here!

It's interesting to see how all the news talk about the low level of confidence in America right now is continuing to lower that confidence.

When everyone goes into "Duck and Cover" mode, there's nobody out looking for the opportunities that inevitably arise out of turmoil.

Aristotle's top virtue: Courage. Harry Potter's top quality: Courage. What every Cowardly Lion needs right now: Courage!

Every evening Emperor Marcus Aurelius asked himself: What have I learned today? And he wrote it down. His notes on life: The Meditations.

Emotion is a weakness only if it takes control of you and causes you to act inconsistently with your beliefs and values.

We should be careful with generalizations – which reminds me of the old saying: "All generalizations are false, including this one."

Random Insights – Wis[...]
And Walking Yo[...]

"Anyone wh[...]
is, forsooth[...]

A gre[...]
are[...]

"It is always the adventurers who accompli[...] g
- Montesquieu

What attitude toward life do I find ideal in people? I should do my best to bring that attitude to each day.

Read Beowulf. Good insights: The proud warrior flies solo. He never changes with age, never partners with others. He goes down in flames.

Another good read: Gilgamesh. Bad leader does wrong, meets his equal, confronts mortality – alters his perspective. Ends up great.

Fear, being natural – it's just up to us what we do with it. Do we always give in to it, or courageously resist it with good reason?

Had a nice exercise walk. Fed a swan a hotdog bun. Watched a bunch of ducks. Birds were auditioning for Neighborhood Idol. Restful.

If I can stretch my conception of work enough to cover Twitter, then tweeting has turned me into a serious workaholic. Help me.

By the way, we should be wary of quotes we see here attributed to great people past. A spurious Plato made the rounds yesterday.

quoteth me from a social networking source
being insufficiently cautious." - Shakespeare

philosopher of the past said: "Be at least who you
Be recognizable!" Be consistent!

Camus: "One must not cut oneself off from the world. No
one who lives in the sunlight makes a failure of his life."
(Notebooks, May 1935)

"Don't give way to conformity and to office hours. Don't
give up. Never give up – always demand more." Camus,
Notebooks (Oct 20, 1937)

Plato worried about this: The paradox of how to get beyond
what you know, when that limits what you can see. Where is
the path?

The answer lies in nearly constant exploration and exposure.
We go where our light takes us, and as we step, the light expands.

Just saw Shatner's post on Boston Legal. As a philosopher, I
prosecute falsehood and defend truth. Denny Crane.

A great dinner doesn't have to be expensive. But it can cap
the day in a metaphysical way.

Good morning, early bird tweeters. "This is the day that the
Lord has made, let us rejoice and be glad in it." Biblical caffeine.

Toga all bunched up this morning. Shaking the cobwebs out of the
neural webs. Can feel brain regions sequentially going online...

Socrates: "The unexamined life is not worth living." But, of course,
the unlived life is not worth examining! So Live The Day!

Invest thinking time into the early part of the day. Be strategic. Little things add up, and big things multiply!

Thought for the day: "Pursue worthy aims." - Solon (600 BC)

"It is terrifying to see how easily, in certain people, all dignity collapses." Albert Camus, even without the benefit of reality TV.

I tweeted this with a fountain pen.

I always wondered why people often omit vowels here. So it's for Retweet purposes! Ancient Hebrews must have had some version of Twitter.

Tweeted this with #2 pencil. Erasing is tougher.

"Great necessities call out great virtues." - Abigail Adams

Abigail once more: "The habits of a vigorous mind are formed in contending with difficulties."

Some say that dealing with difficulties makes us smarter.

Avoiding difficulties may then make us dumber – if I understand that at all.

The smarter you are, the more you're able to avoid difficulties, but the more difficulties you avoid, the dumber you are?

Academic articles can be hard to read. But with great people in any field, if you master the lingo, you get big payoff.

Professors aren't usually taught to be great communicators. That's why great teachers are rare, and good academic writers are, too.

With great contemporary philosophy writing, you can work and work till your head hurts, and then, a new vista opens beyond imagination.

The Availability Fallacy: If it's true, it ought to be obvious. Some things are accessible only to those who cultivate the ability to see.

On the other hand, obscurity is not the same thing as profundity, but often a mask of its lack.

Sorry, I don't mean to go all Yoda on you. Or: I don't all Yoda on you mean to go.

Not many following these posts, so I think I have a highbrow group here. The Twitter-elite!

The power of exuberance is without clear limit.

Loved an old dog on a walk tonight. Gave him a Milk-bone. Made his day. Mine too. Walking daily in hopes of being an old dog myself.

Lost a follower today. Would have given him a Milk-bone, or a biscuit of wisdom, at least. Invite him back, if you see him.

Often I regret how succinct we have to be here. I try to build these tweets to have more depth than they appear to hold.

We're all philosophers, "lovers of wisdom" to some extent. We search for insight, and it moves us forward.

Getting ready for my philosophy fix of the week, Jack Bauer. I wrote the Foreword to the book 24 and Philosophy, in case you see it. Fun!

Perfect balance is not an option: It's a dynamic process of correction and re-correction. It's a bit like a dance.

Our need to create meaning has been heightened by tech and speed. Before, meaning was largely pre-made, unchanging.

My parents were born into a pre-made thought universe in 1920s North Carolina. Now, we're born into a wild bazaar of ideas and possibilities.

We're all forced into more blank sheet thinking. And as Mondrian once said, confronted with a blank canvas, the hardest stroke is the first.

"Do not be concerned with what others have or have not done. Observe your own actions and inactions." – Dhammapada

It's interesting how many ancients said the same things. It's almost as if they were all retweeting each other.

So many of my best thoughts were stolen by the great thinkers of the past. They got away with it only because I hadn't been born yet.

For me, a new user, the cool thing about Twitter is the sense of instant real time connection with people you'd otherwise not know.

And where else can you go to always get a blast of positive energy first thing in the day?

Twitter is a different tool to different people: Like a tech-friendly Swiss Army Knife for the soul.

Had leftovers for lunch. Had to say that after reading lunch tweets today from great cafes in major world cities. The leftovers were good!

Now that I think of it, many of my tweets are about great leftovers – the wisdom nuggets of the past. They improve with age.

But then, to beat the metaphor to death, we don't always have to dine with famous chefs. Sometimes, what we cook up for each other is great.

I think we're here to give more than we get, which is an impossible task, since the more we give, the more yet we get. And that's the point!

Maytag just recalled 1.6 million refrigerators. That repairman is finally going to be really busy.

Just learned the word 'business' comes from the Old English 'bisignis' which meant, "anxiety, unease, and distress." Ha!

A family member suggested that the glacial pace with which I'm drawing followers in my 2 weeks here says it's not for me. Hope conquers all.

Today's market was a glimmer. Whether a false start or the beginning, there will be a turnaround, to new and exciting things in America.

The economy is redefining. And we get to see it. How great is that? Better: We get to help make it happen. And that's actually the best.

Toss your pebble into the pond. You never know how far the ripples will go!

Just because the market is down doesn't mean that lives and dreams are over! People prevail!

The Stoics saw life as a party we're invited to attend. We'll enjoy it while we're here. And when it ends, we won't overstay our welcome.

The Stoic view is wise deep down, at least when you're not too deeply down.

Is it my imagination, or could it actually be that whenever I tweet, my follower number goes down by one? I guess silence is golden!

Philosophy helps us understand how to set our goals in areas where we have some control and build out from there.

Inner strength is the only reliable source of outer strength.

Inner resilience is the only reliable source of outer results.

It's interesting to see how gamesmanship can flourish anywhere: here, in the constant quest for numbers.

You know me, when I lose one "Follower" I want to go find him and see what went wrong in our Twitterelationship.

All the great wisdom traditions have stressed Paying Attention!

Everything past has prepared you for this day!

The fullness of the day that awaits us is immeasurable. Pluck the ripe fruit of possibility and enjoy it!

Good morning, friends. How is everything in your neighborhood of Twitteropolis?

The sweet tweets of the day, with rosy fingered dawn, welcome us all again to the great field of incredible potential.

Everything we've ever experienced has prepared us for today.

Cloudy skies this morning at the beach lead me into a little silly smile therapy to get the brain juice mixed just right.

I love ambiguous headlines: "Innovations to Selectively Kill Cancer Cells" – I say: Kill 'em all!

Philosophy of the day: The best of pure possibility becomes reality only through us!

During this economic downturn, I see a spiritual upturn, and it bodes well for us all.

Your distinctive genius awaits its full realization, and that requires action each day.

Someone just asked what philanthropy really is.

Etymologically, phil means "love of," and anthropos means "humankind." Philanthropy is an expression of love for people, nothing less!

The secret act of kindness is one of the deepest spiritual acts!

Many people now see ethics as about staying out of trouble; they don't realize it's about creating strength!

Call at home: Flight cancelled. 10 minutes to pack! Drove 2 hours to alt airport, got here in time for a backup delayed for hours!

Pascal: Most of our troubles arise from the fact that we don't know how to sit quietly in our rooms. But most good stuff too!

I'm sitting in the RDU airport, US Airways Club, and hoping for the best. I guess it won't be dinner at the Ritz tonight!

Somebody tweet weather.com and get them to do something about the weather rather than just talking about it!

Expect the unexpected! Plan for the unplanned! And find a way to enjoy the process as it goes!

Following my own advice: Enjoying a bountiful repast of US Airways crackers and cheese, with a cranberry nut mix at my table for one.

Truth is the foundation of possibility: Reality provides and we decide.

What is truth? It's a multifaceted target easy to miss and hard to hit – but necessary to use in support of our dreams.

Full moon over Manhattan: all the buildings of smart, energetic, hard working people – a visual reminder that the economy will return.

It's been a beautiful night of flying up the east coast of America. The wonders of flight can inspire.

Plato's Cave: In chains, most see shadows on the wall and think them realities. The only path from the cave to freedom is courage.

The primary virtue is courage. Without it, we won't live any of the other virtues!

When you wish upon a star: Why is it that some phrases we have to sing? And singing helps us remember!

Life is a song. And we're all the singers.

It is in a flash that we expand. Sameness takes time. Creativity happens in a moment!

I've been on Twitter only a short time, and you guys already give me the strength and inspiration to make a difference in our tough time!

You are making the future.

Even if we don't know the reason we're here, we can take the hints we get and make a real difference!

You are appreciated!

If words were love, our 140 block would expand to fill the page! Let the best tweets expand and grow to fill your heart!

Launch some love into the world today, tweeters!

"Whatever we recognize in a person, we inflame in him." - Nietzsche. So praise someone's goodness today – fan the flame!

Someone mentioned phronesis yesterday – Aristotle's concept of practical wisdom: The ability to set proper goals and pursue them well.

Wisdom is an art, not just a collection of insights derived from that art. And an art must be practiced.

Practice wisdom today and prosper!

Your faith is your transcendent guidance system that keeps you from having to make up everything from scratch!

In every way, faith at its best is the assurance that things aren't always what they appear.

Each day is fresh beginnings and, sometimes, in surprising ways.

Heraclitus: You can't step into the same river twice, since new waters flow on.

Heraclitus: Things are always changing.

Heraclitus once more: Character is destiny!

I'm having lunch surrounded by beauty, overlooking the Statue of Liberty. They've even put a telescope in my room. Great view of the lady!

It was a very nice gift from France, and it keeps on inspiring us all this time later.

Bring hot coals together, and they light a flame! Apart, they grow cold. Let's flame together today!

Ironing clothes. Just walked around the hotel room looking for the pants I was wearing. Not yet at Socrates' level, but well on my way!

Speaking of flaming together today, I'd better go turn off the iron.

The Statue of Liberty recalls Viktor Frankl's insight: The one liberty that can never be taken away is the freedom to choose our attitudes.

The Lady is holding her flame high to remind us of our freedom, and to spur us on to its proper use.

Loving what you do is so vital. I found myself laughing out loud twice today just by myself, at the sheer fun of it all.

Watching The Office, then 30 Rock. I love Alec Baldwin's character – in the theatrical sense, of course.

The 140 limit is like eating all your meals on a very small plate. It's good discipline. But I often sneak away and pig out.

Twitter is a world unto itself. You see people you know from the "outside world" but it's just a different experience.

One thing I will say about Twitter is that I haven't had a bad experience yet, in two weeks – just good stuff.

Having room service breakfast before LaGuardia. A full moon sits right over the Statue of Liberty. What a great sight this morning!

"No wind blows fair for a ship that has no port" - Seneca. Let's have clear goals and aims for this day!

Talked to guys yesterday who saw the US Airways plane land in the Hudson. They all thought, "This can't turn out well."

Many went home as soon as they could to avoid seeing the results. Most had witnessed 9-11 from their office windows across the street.

They said they couldn't take watching another tragedy. Life sometimes surprises us. What happened of course was a triumph.

Expect good things on this day! And, most of all: Do something good.

"The first thing people need when they get up each morning is hope." - Rudy Pensa (Rudy's Guitar Stop on 48th Street)

Self-giving is self-fulfilling.

I overheard something great in Charlotte while in line to board a San Diego Flight. It reminds us to make sure we're communicating well.

Little girl, pointing: "Momma, where is that man going." "The same place we're going, honey." Pause to ponder. "To Aunt Judy's house?"

Clarity communicates without confusion.

Wisdom is one part thought, two parts action.

Book Recommendation: Mary Shelley's Frankenstein – One of the greatest cautionary tales ever for smart high achievers.

It's amazing the number of small kindnesses you can witness each day if you really look.

Socrates taught Plato, who taught Aristotle, who taught Alexander the Great, when he was just Alexander the Average. Greatness multiplies.

Every day's a great day on this side of the grass!

Courage is the only path to your best personal future.

Gratitude is the only way to walk your path.

Companionship is the only thing that can make the journey rich!

I am now two followers away from hitting 200. For many of you that experience is ancient history. For a newbie, it's a biggie!

The Few, The Proud, the Philosophers!

I had fun yesterday with some of the top financial advisors in the country. They had a very positive attitude, and were a joy.

Chewy granola bars have cosmic powers unknown to science.

One of the strongest powers in our lives, and a major obstacle to our goals, is self-deception. Always beware!

The small things make a big difference over time, and in not as much time as we'd think!

At its best, doing philosophy live and in person is like jazz. It's an art form. But then, really, what isn't?

I realized early on that writing is a form of thinking. I clarify things by writing. It's a cognitive discipline that can benefit others.

Between Twitter and Hulu, and email overload, it's amazing that I'm gainfully employed at all.

Sympathy is a great moral quality; empathy is even more intimately connected.

Just by being alive, we make a contributive difference – is it for good or ill? That's up to us.

If you're feeling pathetic, go get empathetic, and your feelings will suddenly change.

Empathy is an inherently motivational experience. When you really feel what another is going through, it's hard not to act and help.

So much of what breaks us down at first, opens us up in the end.

A dream is all imagination, a desire is simply inclination – a goal is a commitment of the will.

"Attitude not aptitude determines altitude": Don't sigh when you try, and fly high?

William James saw that all champions have one thing in common – Precursive Faith, the ability to "run ahead of" the available evidence.

The evidence of the past is never sufficient to prove the success of the future: Champions don't let that hold them back!

.

Personality and Character, Appearance and Reality

"People are always telling you who they are." Steven Spielberg. – Listen carefully!

Never waste an opportunity to learn something new.

Throughout my day, I like to engage people in conversation – I can learn so much!

Wisdom is almost always about putting things into perspective.

If I had to pick my favorite Roman Stoic and Practical Philosopher, it would be hard, but it might have to be Seneca.

The Stoics write as if they were alive now and experiencing all our problems and opportunities. They knew human nature.

The Stoics understood that only inner strength can prevail against the challenges of life.

Marcus Aurelius: A great leader's inner power. Epictetus: The path to liberation. Seneca: The full and happy life.

Courage is not an absence of fear, but a source for positive and definite action despite it.

Aristotle saw courage as a midpoint between timidity and temerity – neither reticent nor rash, the brave soul takes measured action for good.

I love this: "Anything worth doing is worth doing badly." Don't wait for perfect – get going. We learn by doing, says Aristotle!

Bermuda has never had a festival just for short films. Was it because they couldn't think of a snappy name?

Words rarely used in conversation these days, in ordinary settings: 'Wisdom' and 'Virtue'. Wonder why?

The least important things, we think about and talk about the most. The most important things, we think about and talk about the least. Socrates

I hope you didn't miss all my wise and scintillating explorations of the human spirit this morning. Wait – that was someone else.

Everything worthwhile is easier said than done. This is part of what gives it value.

It's time for some lunch! Chicken nuggets now – wisdom nuggets later. Y'all talk among yourselves. I'll be back.

One of the greatest mistakes of the past half-century has been to confuse personality with character.

Personality is style. Character is substance.

Personality is The How. Character is The Who.

Personality may get you in the door, but character will keep you going.

Personality is the expression on your face. Character is the attitude in your heart.

Somebody stop me.

Personality is the dance. Character is the music.

I'm trying to restrain myself.

Personality is the marketing. Character is the product.

Personality is the foam. Character is the beer.

Tough crowd.

Personality is the headline. Character is the story.

Tap. Tap. Hello? Is this on? Can you hear me in the back?

Oh! You're all listening in rapt and silent contemplation? Good!

Personality is what you show. Character is what you grow.

There are also connections between character and personality.

Some of the most deeply attractive of personality traits are an overflow of real character.

One thing I hate about doing anything that takes me away from these discussions here is that I can't watch them later on Hulu!

Just when we thought evolution was safe to teach, we see the devolution of everything around us.

I tried to buy Rodney Dangerfield's new book – they wouldn't take my credit card. I get no respect, no respect at all.

If no one ever spoke unless he knew what he was talking about, a terrible hush would descend on the world. - Who said that?

Corundum, under pressure and heat, becomes sapphires and rubies. With a small variation in conditions, it becomes the material of sandpaper.

Either way, heat and pressure result in beauty or usefulness.

A small difference in the process can make a big difference in the results.

This is the conundrum of corundum.

I got that information out of a complex little account in this month's Yale Alumni Magazine. Boola!

Requesting clearance to land at Twitterboro.

Just finished writing follow up emails to clients from this week. I think follow up notes are so important.

I like to write notes in fountain pen when I can, but the monitor screen keeps smearing up so badly.

Socrates mastered irony. I've mastered ironing! Ugly wrinkles are my enemy: In clothes, arguments, and my face.

I have ironed clothes in almost every four and five star resort in America – living the glamorous life.

There are a few great hotels where I've actually never been wrinkled.

Someone's reporting from a major film festival that Gary V the wine guy is sick. And he's scheduled to speak.

Tell Gary he has to SWALLOW the cold medicine, not just swish and spit it.

Half the time he just sniffs it and writes notes. TAKE THE TYLENOL, don't just get enthusiastic about the ruby color!

A Shout Out to the good people who have chosen to follow me here! You are geniuses of perceptive discernment, and I honor you.

Or, you may be like visitors at the zoo, who have heard about the caged philosopher. In either case, I appreciate you!

Typos are the bane of fast tweets. It's like a paint smear on a work of art. Of course, if the art is mostly paint smears, that's different.

Are fortune cookies any better or worse than meteorologists, economists, and the CIA?

Ok, I'll say good day to all, and to all a good night. Someone turn out the lights when you're done, OK?

"Small opportunities are often the beginning of great enterprises." – Demosthenes

Aristotle said if you want a happy life, it helps to get born to the right parents. That was wise, but as advice, hard to use.

Wilmington is grey and cloudy, misty, atmospheric. Makes me want to make a movie.

Happy Sunday! A day for great things!

General Recommendation: Trade Paperback: Superman for All Seasons, by Jeph Loeb and Tim Sale, a great team also on Batman.

When I read Superman for All Seasons, I remember anew why I'm willing to leave family and home to help others.

Wittgenstein: We mistake the limits of our vision for the limits of the world.

"Appearances are often deceiving." – Aesop

"Things often love to conceal their true nature." – Heraclitus

'Twixt optimist and pessimist the difference is droll. The optimist sees the doughnut, the pessimist, the hole. M. Wilson

Ok I'm getting carried away with quotations!

In a few minutes, I'm going to go out and walk in the mist before the rain comes. It makes me feel like Bogey.

I once rode in a 1940s Grumman Mallard Seaplane that had been dredged up from Tokyo Harbor. It was such a Bogart ride!

Here's looking at you, Tweeters!

There is this old Jewish concept – biblical, actually: The presentness of the past. We are because it is. And it endures.

Given the vastness of space and the immensity of time, abundance is a natural concept – but only when we open our hearts.

I was being cosmic there for a moment because of an abundance quote that popped onto my screen.

We should come up with a new pair of concepts to explore today, like character and personality yesterday.

How about appearance and reality? They're similar, but broader.

Appearance is the shell. Reality is the egg.

Appearance is the peel. Reality is the banana.

Appearance is the sizzle. Reality is the steak.

Appearance is surface. Reality is depth.

Appearance is cosmetic. Reality is cosmic.

Appearance is the light. Reality is the sun.

Appearance is quick. Reality is long.

Appearance is seen. Reality is searched.

Ok, Enough! Or: Maybe not.

Appearance is enough for the many. Reality is enough for the few. Hey, that's a good one.

Appearance is completely empirical. Reality is just so metaphysical.

Unless, like Bishop Berkeley, you do believe that to be is to be perceived – in which case, we all need paparazzi.

Appearance is that I have an endless number of aphorisms here. Reality is that I don't.

"Always look beyond the first right answer." I love that! It was always the kid sitting two desks away who had the BEST answer.

Sitting here singing "Tweet Home, Alabama."

I just got my first tweet in Russian. I'm not Russian to respond. I have no idea what it means – the Wonder of Twitter.

Gaily bedight, a gallant knight, in sunshine and in shadow, had journeyed long, singing a song, in search of Twitterado.

Forgive the free association – it IS FREE, after all.

If today is the first day of the rest of your life, it's also the last day of the first of your life. Half Full? Half Empty? Half Baked?

Difficulty gives all things their value. – Montaigne

To say is easy; to do is hard. In a world of great talkers – be a great doer!

Talk is cheap (unless you have the wrong cell plan); action is costly.

Advice of the day: Encourage quality everywhere!

The world is in a mess right now. Our best efforts are needed!

There's a lot of faux philosophy around! Superficial advice. Empty cheerleading. True wisdom is exciting enough! No need to cavort in Hype!

There is in the world faux wisdom, faux virtue, faux almost anything. Test everything.

Ben Bernanke: "How do you get confidence, that's the question." The answer is that courage moves forward and creates confidence.

The biggest problem in the world right now may be a lack of trust based on a lack of truth.

Every downturn has preceded an upturn. This one will, too.

The cool thing about philosophy: Not letting appearances deceive us – plumbing the depths, and seeking the essence of any situation!

The true philosopher is a detective, an investigator, a relentless questioner of reality. Each of us can take up this role!

Lots of successful people come to fear failure, and so limit their future success.

Aristotle taught me that happiness is an activity: A dynamic engagement, involvement, or participation in the best of life.

Emerson believed in experiments and looked forward to surprises. How many nice surprises do we give ourselves?

Good friends Ford, Edison, and Firestone constantly invented things to change the world. Makes me regret I watch so much TV.

Of course, Socrates didn't watch TV and he never got anything written. Neither did Epictetus.

The old adage: It's better to be silent and thought ignorant than to open your mouth and prove it.

You tweeps have helped make it a great day here in TomV-Morrisland. I want to say thanks.

Gotta go soon, so someone remember to close up shop here, Ok?

Just on to say good morning: then off to get work done. But I'll be back to share the bounty of the day!

As Homer would say, Rosy fingered dawn calls us on to new adventures!

Not Homer Simpson: He'd just day "D'Oh!"

Courage is a midpoint between cowardice and craziness. It's always the wise path forward.

I have ambitious plans for the day! It's rainy and so I won't be as tempted to go out and play!

Our potential awaits only our wise action!

The conversational flow here can take us away from our ticking inner clocks of productivity! Be aware!

For me, a morning cup 'o Twitter is just the thing to jump start the neurons for the day!

A squirrel sits ten feet away watching me as he eats his peanut butter and corn meal breakfast. Birds are singing him through the feast.

Morning is a call to action! A promise of new things! A foretaste of the day! The starting gate of a span of time we'll never have again.

By the end of this week, let's all be able to look back with satisfaction on what we've experienced and done.

"People wish to be settled; only as far as they are unsettled is there any hope for them." Emerson ("Circles")

"Life is a series of surprises." Emerson

It may still be dark wherever you are. Don't worry – you can create light as you go.

"Beware when the great God lets loose a thinker on this planet. Then all things are at risk." Emerson

"The universe is fluid and volatile." Emerson again!

One more Emerson thought today: "Be a gift and a benediction."

My four-year-old granddaughter just asked where I was going. I said "crazy" and she gave me a real look!

Oh, national news! Back in thirty minutes. Talk amongst yourselves.

Hang in there. Most difficult things get worse before they get better!

Had a great day, got a lot done, now watching a Seinfeld rerun. I like to balance serious reflection and mindless mirth.

You guys! I've realized that Aristotle is "Too big to fail." So someone send a stimulus package! I'll make sure it's used well.

"In giving advice, seek to help, not to please, your friend." - Solon (c. 600 BC)

One more Saying from Solon this morning – the hardest advice for me: "Nothing too much."

"Prefer a loss to a dishonest gain: The one brings pain for a moment, the other for all time." Chilon

I'm quoting some of the Lesser Known Philosophers today, just to get them equal time here with Emerson and Zig Ziglar!

Uh Oh. "Gesticulating in speaking should be avoided, as a mark of insanity." Chilon again, and this time he's wrong, or I'm nuts!

Pittacus: "Cherish truth, fidelity, skill, cleverness, sociability, carefulness."

One more Pittacus goodie: "Know your opportunity."

I was going to try to quote Hegel here, but the first subordinate clause of any remark of his runs at least ten times our limit.

Hope you're catching my quotes from obscure old philosophers today. What's old is ever new again.

Being asked what is sweet to human beings, Bias (of Priene) – one of the 7 Sages of Ancient Greece – answered: Hope.

You guys just gave me my first real laugh of the day. Job done. Now you can take some time off.

My guide to the power of distraction is Pascal. We need to simplify! The kudzu of commitments easily takes over!

Bias again: "Be slow to undertake a new enterprise, but persevere in it steadily once it's launched." Slow now means: think a minute first.

I like that old philosopher a lot, but that just may be a Bias of mine.

Remember today the Four Foundations of greatness: Truth, Beauty, Goodness, and Unity!

I almost ran into The Thinker in a great art museum. Rushed around a corner, BOOM! He's a very muscular guy.

Rodin had the perfect blend: The man of thought is a man of action.

But the question remains: What is The Thinker thinking? "Wonder where I left my clothes?"

Cleobulus Leads Off – More Insights on Reality, Patience, and Smiles

Cleobulus: "Set your mind on something good." How's that for obscure and great?

"Know how to bear the changes of fortune with nobility." Cleobulus again

Socrates, Plato, Aristotle … Cleobulus?

Cleobulus Love-Fest Continued: "Seek virtue, avoid vice." Simple. Difficult. Vital.

One more from Cleo: "Moderation is the best thing." Where else would you get this stuff?

Every great plan starts with "Where We Are Now" defines "Where We Want to Go" and develops "What We Need to Do to Get There."

Guard your mind as you would you wallet. There's a lot more of value in there!

Crime News! Target thief confronts security guard with affordable designer cutlery.

The greatest good is not to get all that you want, but to want all the right things. – Menedemus. (Yes, THAT Menedemus.)

As you age, your memory gets like a really popular nightclub that's hard to get into, with big burly bouncers ejecting patrons at will.

Once in the Costa Rica cloud forest, I had the thought that we don't know one percent of anything now about how nature could help us!

As we age, maybe our skin wrinkles just to give us the extra room to spread our wings.

Off to work out! See you all on the flip side! Remember, Twitter Quotes are only as good as what we do with them!

"Success is attained when a man does what he aims at, in the right way, as becomes a good man." Plato

Do you own any things that make you pause during this recession? I have an expensive pair of shoes I'm almost afraid to wear.

Maybe that's why Socrates went around barefoot.

I've had such a busy afternoon I couldn't tweet! The cosmic injustice of it all!

"We should call no man happy until he's dead." - Many Ancient Greeks With Clearly Odd Standards.

It's been a great day of good lessons. Almost everything takes more time or money than you'd think.

Everything worth doing is worth working for!

I pour my heart into everything I do!

Aristotle saw wittiness and practical intelligence as basic human virtues. He would have loved to see so much of both on Twitter.

"A joyful heart is good medicine for the soul!" Proverbs

I see lots of familiar faces here this morning! And you are all SMILING!

This is a new day of challenge, laughter, joy, work, play, and tweeting!

Dreaming is good. It can even be impressive, but it's action that does the real work!

The worse things get, the more of an optimist I become. People can tolerate the terrible, but the intolerable wakes us all up to action!

No jumping on the Twitter sofas! I'll be back and I want to see this place looking nice!

Those dark clouds on the horizon just mean refreshing rain for what you want to grow!

I think it was Abigail Adams who said, "In difficult times, good men shine." Good women, too!

Swimming against the current beats floating away face down any day.

Once I leave this wonderful visit to Twitterville, it's laser focus time!

I'll make it a positive day by being creative and collaborative – the two secrets to dealing with challenge!

There is nothing more important than this day. Relish it, and use it well!

Remember Plato's Cave! Don't spend the day spelunking there, but escape the shadows into the light!

I approach the banquet of this day hungry and thirsty for the best it offers! Come join me!

Alexander the Great conquered the world at age thirty. Are you just getting started? There's a lot to look forward to!

"Let us rejoice in life!" Ralph Waldo Emerson

I dealt with a surly customer service guy today, and treated his neglect and hostility with kindness and consideration.

It's sad to see someone in a starting position at a level of irritable incompetence. But I tried to lift him up.

Sometimes rude people enter our lives just to give us the opportunity to exercise compassion.

It's said of Emerson: "He seldom felt he had made the fullest possible use of a day."

Every minute today is precious! That's why I have to spend a few of them here throughout the day! You guys always show me something good.

"Nothing great was ever accomplished without enthusiasm!" Emerson

"The ideas in every man's mind make him who he is." Emerson again

"I am defeated all the time; yet to victory I am born." I wish I could stop quoting Emerson.

Can you tell what I've been reading today? Ralph Waldo it is. He traveled the country philosophizing in his time, as I do in ours.

One more thought before lunch: The real question is not "What can I know?" but "How should I live?"

I currently hold some false beliefs. My friends and critics can help me spot them.

I currently have some flaws. Other people can help me see them.

Seek to live not the most pleasant, but the very best, life you can.

"Nothing will ever satisfy greed, but a little is enough for nature's need." Seneca

"Life is long enough ... for the accomplishment of the greatest things if the whole of it is well invested." Again, Seneca

I realized today: Some people enjoy the benefits of high self-esteem largely because of exceeding low standards.

Your life now is a bright and remarkable challenge suspended between two eternities.

There will never be another day exactly like this one. Make the most of it every hour.

Each of us is born with the tools of self-transformation. Use them well today!

A little early morning philosophy is bracing! It's a very good prep for the world that awaits us!

Let's all splash the cold water of energizing insight on our faces! Awake for the day!

It's not that we don't know what we need to know, we just need to be reminded of what we do know and need to do!

I tried to tweet Schopenhauer this morning. I'm not sure he ever had a 140 character thought.

I just found one! "Intellect is invisible to the man who has none." - Happily Visible Arthur Schopenhauer

"There is a sense in which we are all alchemists." – Schopenhauer again, and I love it!

We are each dynamos of possibility! We are the transformers of what is!

Pessimism and optimism tend to be self-fulfilling – so why not choose your attitude with this little truth in mind?

We live in a world of appearances – make sure yours represent you well.

Just doing a morning burst of philosophy improvisation here!

You guys inspire me to free form thinking nearly every time I stop by!

Your life is a work of art. Every choice is a stroke on the canvas, a chip in the marble, or a movement in the dance.

Remember: A slow climb beats a fast fall any day!

Got to go take in my toga. You all have a great day! See you later.

Too many of us have lost our concept of "enough."

In ancient warrior cultures, it was a sign of honor for a leader to GIVE AWAY treasure to those who had helped win it.

It's akin to the virtue Aristotle called "Magnificence." – The ability to give on a grand scale – not the ability to take on that scale.

Just slowing down and rolling down the window to wave and shout out some thoughts!

Etymologically, philosophy is just the love of wisdom, or insight for living!

Brevity is the heart of tweetology.

Succinctness is the core of retweeting lore!

Prolixity ends here.

Aristotle: It's not what we own, but who we are, that will last.

Someone has just asked: "What is reality?" I suppose it's safe to ask that question of a philosopher constrained by 140 characters.

Reality is the stubborn underside of appearance.

Reality is a smack on the head, a kick in the pants, or a breeze at your back – depending on the day.

Reality is what you get when you strip away all the illusion.

Hype is what you're promised. Reality is what you get.

Reality is sometimes a rope tossed to a drowning man.

Reality is where the maximal meets the minimal and they both get along.

Reality is where the liberal meets the conservative and each has legitimate concerns.

Reality is a partnership between the outside and the inside.

Reality is the biggest field of possibility there is.

Reality is so great it includes even appearance!

Reality is that I'm hungry and smell something cooking.

The appearance is that someone just called me to dinner – the reality is: I'm going to eat!

Thanks everyone for a great reality romp! Let's play some more, later!

Business is a way of being human. Profit is a side effect of service.

Too many chase transactions, while the wise build relationships!

Failure is a test. Do you rise to the occasion, or fall by the wayside?

I hope we're all doing special things for people during this recession. It's a great time to make a difference.

When I was a professor, all recessions and downturns were rumors. Now that I'm close to the marketplace, I can feel it all.

One thing that I realized anew today is: The Power of Starting.

You know you're doing the right work when you can't tell the difference between work and play!

May today give you Flow from the top of your head to the soles of your feet!

Success often breeds an unconscious sense of entitlement – Never let that hold you back!

Our biggest help or hindrance over which we have control is attitude.

Conversation is the life force of Twitterville.

Be a change agent for good today!

Light a fire for the higher values today! Soothe someone's concern. Inspire someone's action. Lead the way in joyous exaltation!

The one thing that seems completely free is actually the most valuable thing of all – your time.

Laughter is so important to me each day. I sometimes find myself laughing aloud at myself!

"States are doomed when they are unable to distinguish good men from bad." - Antisthenes (a student of Socrates)

It was once said to Antisthenes: "Many men praise you." His reply: "Why? What have I done wrong?"

The many live with illusion. The few appreciate truth.

"It's better to be with a handful of good men fighting all the bad, than with a host of the bad against a handful of the good." – Antisthenes once more

The trouble with treating other people as equals is that before you know it, they're doing the same thing to you. Peter Devries from memory.

Went to the grocery store and bought "Blood Oranges." Wow! What a color inside! Intense Prince purple!

One day I got two checks: A year's royalties on a philosophy book, $34.95; Payment for a two-sentence book cover blurb, $250.

I remember saying, "Ok, from now on, it's blurbs only."

No wonder the great thinkers did so many short "quotes" – I bet they cleaned up!

"I never really said anything important, but people still quote me so much." – Anonymous

How to Increase Your Wealth Using Twitter! – Since it's free, any hour you're on here, you're not out spending money. And that can add up.

Success makes too many people take things for granted. Don't let it do this to you.

Almost everything worth doing is an art – we can get better at it with the right efforts over time.

It's a bad head cold day, with lots of oranges and antihistamines. I'm afraid to write anything in my haze.

Of course haze never stopped many writers in the past.

Haze may even have made some careers.

I'm actually going to be able to do some work today: Low-key work and philosophical work. But work, nonetheless.

I exemplify an old Hindu proverb: I can't tell the difference between work and play most days.

Some claim they can't tell the difference between "He's a philosopher," and "He's one sick dude."

Twitter is the perfect place for sick people. No more demanding that what we can accomplish – 140 and send.

A virtue (Latin 'virtu') is a form of strength. I see patience as a strength, and thus as a virtue.

The Tao Te Ching has good insight about the importance of patience.

Sometimes, we need to act. Other times, we need to refrain from acting.

Sometimes, we need to press on. Other times, we need to hang back.

Wisdom is the ability to judge what's right in any given situation – when it's right to do, and when it's right to allow.

Patience is the inner discipline that allows us to conform our wills to the timing of the world.

Patience is the skill of dancing to the subtle music of life, and not getting awkwardly ahead.

Patience is what allows us to accept any rhythm that's not at first our own.

Patience is the awareness and acceptance that not everything and everyone is yet ripe.

Good riffing. This is why philosophers have always benefited from traveling in groups. Not to mention group discounts.

I love nonsense. How otherwise could I have gotten through graduate school?

Thirty-six publishers turned down my first book. Good thing there was a thirty-seventh in existence at the time! Patience paid off!

When people reject you, it's not always about you – it's often about them.

Movers and shakers are called that because we upset the inertia of the world.

Be an unorthodox force for good today!

Upend the wrong side-up things of the world!

Whenever anyone gives me an "attitude," I like to give one back that comes with a genuine smile.

A smile can be an act of compassion in the face of a need, or a delicious enjoyment of the absurd.

I love a smile that's an upwelling of inner joy, the glee that spills out through the face!

The magnetism of a real smile can't be fully explained, just enjoyed.

And happy laughter is the best music of the soul.

A smile can honor, celebrate, and invite. And a real smile always involves.

Nothing deflects and dissolves bad feeling like a smile.

Of course, a malefactor can smile manipulatively.

A villain can smile perversely. But there is something very different about it.

Everything genuine can be counterfeited. In human emotions, only wisdom can tell the difference.

Has anyone else noticed how symbolism is trumping substance almost everywhere in our culture right now?

My life is sometimes long stretches of indolence punctuated by intense bursts of activity.

The indolence allows for contemplation, the activity allows for sharing it.

Philosopher and novelist Iris Murdoch said that when decision time comes, most of our choices are already made by our values.

Confession is a form of cleansing. It's a way of hitting the "restart" button.

An apology, at its best, is an act of moral courage.

Forgiveness can be an act of moral leadership.

I'm spending more time on the practical philosophers these days, squeezing their insights for our time.

Every drop of wisdom helps.

The biggest challenge for many people is adapting when things aren't working.

I'm asking: What have I done? What have I left undone? Who have I helped? What have I learned?

I'll welcome tomorrow with gratitude, courage, and the intent to enjoy myself while getting things done!

Let the four foundations of great relationships guide you in everything: Truth, Beauty, Goodness, and Unity!

Wellbeing is attained little by little, yet it is no little thing itself. – Zeno

I'm not yet where I want to be, but I'm not still where I used to be, and I make a little progress every day!

When the birds sing to you today, sing back!

Some days the mind wakes up the body, other days the body is well on its way before the mind joins the party!

To learn something new is great – to live it and pass it on is even greater!

My Dad: Do something as long as you love it and have something to contribute. If that changes, you should make a change.

Signing off for now! Back Later: Your Conceptual Cowboy, your avid aphorist, your epideictic epigrammatist.

Fear keeps us on our toes. But then so does ballet. Maybe that's why I fear ballet. No, it's more likely the tights.

Courage isn't an immunity to fear, but a proper response to it.

With any list of ways to get what you want, add one of ways to get what you need, and of ways to enjoy what you have!

St. Augustine's mother taught him that getting what we want is easy compared to learning what we should want!

Relationships rule the world!

Singing back to the birds, shining back at the sun, giving back to our friends makes us partners with the best in our world.

The power of inertia is subtle and strong – that's how it holds us back.

We're waxing wise about life, which is painless and effective, and smoothes out the surface of our existence.

"He has the most who is most content with the least." Diogenes. But then again, he can often do the best who is best prepared with the most!

I'm a little cynical about cynicism these days.

It's nice to have a business that's first a mission, then a commercial enterprise. I feel very blessed by it.

The focused mind can attain great things. Our main obstacle is distraction.

Many futurists claim an ability that almost everyone wants and no one seems to have.

But lots of futurists have had a bad track record. That's one reason they focus us on the future, not the past!

Time is strange. The past is no longer, the future is not yet, and the present is of no duration.

To live the present well, we have to dig deep into it and expand it!

Hope, not hype, is a basic human need.

The great gifts of love and death have in common that they teach us to let go, release, and accept unconditionally.

The superficial opposites of death and love show us our place in reality like nothing else. They will teach us if we will learn.

We Are Co-Creators of the Possible, Personal Cauldrons of Potential

We are all explorers of the possible, and co-creators of it as well!

We are the sum total of our experiences, augmented by our dreams and our actions.

"Philosophy is the highest music." Plato. But then music may be the highest philosophy.

"Most things attributed to me online I never said, including this." - Plato

Ownership is more of a commitment than we realize. To own is to maintain. Things end up owning us!

Hope and coffee always start the day for me! Coffee – so I'm awake enough to hope.

Creativity comes from total immersion and bold openness.

What does a snail riding on the back of a turtle say? "Wheeee!" You don't have to be great to be helpful.

Out the door! Going to breathe the air, sing to some birds, pat an old dog down the street. Keep the insights bubbling!

Take the first step! And then take the second, or else the first will have been wasted!

We never know how things may already be in place to leverage our least actions. So be bold and do!

Sometimes, the simple act of speaking up sets in motion events that you could never have imagined.

We're all somehow less original than we think, and much more than we could have been!

True nobility is unaffected by the apparent indifference of others.

Let's think for a moment about thinking.

Thinking is one of my favorite activities that costs nothing, can be done anywhere, and just may lead to great things.

The paradox of thinking: So easy for those who do it, so hard for those who don't.

Thinking: The one investment that's recession proof!

Thinking: It's not the quantity that counts, but the quality.

Thinking: The one wheel of a cart that, rolling along with Doing, will keep things moving well.

Thinking: The hardest thing in the world to convince people not engaged in it that it's actually a form of work.

Thinking: One of our least popular abilities.

Thinking: One of our least developed skills.

Thinking: Therefore Fully Being.

I see service as a free act of giving, by which we make our difference in the world.

Hope is indeed a fundamental need.

Hype creates false hope. Help creates real hope.

I like to launch the day with a little philosophical improvisation here. It helps jumpstart the higher brain functions!

Keep the wisdom hot and bubbling and I'll be back for a second helping later!

Dogs are pragmatists. Cats are existentialists.

Dogs are egalitarians. Cats are elitists.

The worth of what we do isn't to be measured by the public acclaim we receive. Sometimes, our greatest contributions speak softly.

Socrates' wisdom consisted in humility, self-awareness, and a relentless search for truth.

Prepare to have a Platonic day: In pursuit of the Good.

Also prepare to have an Aristotelian day: In quest of Excellence.

A Platonic day is one inspired by the Good, devoid of illusions, and based on harmony.

An Aristotelian day is one guided by virtue, supported by thought, and productive of happiness.

The thing about Twitter: it's a magical cross between a great conversation, publishing, speaking, and watching a wild TV show.

Live In Pursuit of Wisdom Each Day.

Faith is commitment beyond the range of empirical proof.

Encourage quality wherever it's found. It's an endangered species in our world.

Elevate everyone whose life you touch today. They will benefit, and lift you up as well.

The pragmatic path is to build on what you trust, while stretching to find new truth.

"The heart has its reasons of which reason knows nothing." Pascal

This day has never come before and never will again. Embrace it as the unique gift it is.

I do grin therapy all the time. It works. I may look like an idiot, but I feel great.

Take care of your endorphins, and they'll take care of you. Give them a belly laugh or two.

Me? I love a good belly laugh. I always laugh at my belly.

Heraclitus, revised: "You can't step into the same Twitter steam twice. New tweets are always flowing."

Authenticity is a very important, though secondary, virtue: You wouldn't want to tell a homicidal maniac to, "Just Be Yourself."

Likewise, even the great Golden Rule needs wise application: Otherwise it would turn a masochist into a sadist.

Do unto others as you would have them do unto you.

It's not: Do unto others before they do unto you!

Treat others as you would want to be treated, if you were in their position.

Adaptation is one of our most crucial skills for life.

Sometimes our aspirations will suggest we adapt to the world, just so we can position ourselves eventually to adapt it to our aspirations.

We often even need to adapt how we adapt to change!

Those who aren't adaptive are captive to the past.

The best creation comes through original adaptation.

I change, therefore I am. I am, therefore I change.

We need a transformation in the way we think of transformation.

Sometimes we lead. Sometimes we follow a lead. Our proper responsiveness allows others to respond well, too.

Life is a dance. We lead. We follow. We take our cues from the music. And sometimes we collapse in exhaustion!

Sing your song today. Sing it well and others will join in.

Opposable thumbs help us get things done, opposable people don't.

In the world's wisdom traditions, the greatest consensus on the meaning of life is: Creative love, or loving creativity.

We are here to make a difference in a creative and loving way. Any departure from this is ultimately self-defeating.

Someone asked me earlier whether the philosophers said anything about what it takes for success in anything we do.

Philosophy yields The 7 Cs of Success: Conception, Confidence, Concentration, Consistency, Commitment, Character, and a Capacity to Enjoy.

I want to do what's right, not what's easy; what I feel in my heart, not just what works; what gives others help, and me happiness.

When things are in a big mess, we get to make a big difference!

Encourage wonder when you see it. Dwell in it when you feel it.

You view the present through the lens of the past. But never let that keep you from seeing the future.

When you fill your mind with gratitude, you have no room for the negatives that hold so many back.

Gratitude connects us with the creative flow of life. It allows us to ride on a stream of the world's best energy.

We give each other raw materials for personal reflection and new forms of action.

We're almost perfectly imperfect, nearly completely incomplete, and highly probably improbable.

If the past is any guide to the future, the worst may not be behind us, but the best is yet to come.

Tweet dreams.

Integrity comes from a root word meaning "whole, entire, unified." Integrity means acting with Truth, Beauty, Goodness, and Unity.

Integrity is inner unity, and outer harmony with basic natural laws, duties, and higher values.

Two cups of coffee this morning and there are only scattered neurons firing so far.

Waking up slowly, so as not to frighten any traffic that might be on the neural pathways.

A Twitter friend moves today. Let's all move in support. Let's move our ideas into action, and move on to great things!

The trick for me is to find something each moment that I can attend to and enjoy – Zen mind, Zen move.

Help another person move on to something good.

I come here each morning for soul vitamins! I get my recommended daily dosage real fast!

Pop a few and I'm good!

Today, I'm a morning E-man! – I'm Energetic, Enthusiastic, and Exuberant!

When a problem is so small it's hard to see, it's easy to solve. When it's so big it's easy to see, it's hard to solve.

This is one of the many great insights of the ancients. Early detection and action can together create a solution.

A true leader inspires everyone to run well just to try to keep up!

A friend tweets from his laptop in the hospital delivery room and his wife, with contractions beside him, tweets on her blackberry!

We hope someone has a free hand to actually CATCH THE BABY.

Everything has prepared you for this day!

Life is supposed to be a series of adventures! Enjoy the one you're on today!

Why waste a good day being ordinary?

Why waste a good day worrying about the next one?

It's good to be the best. It's better to be the only. Find your unique niche!

General Life Wisdom: Add pancetta. Or chocolate. But not at the same time.

Got to go deal with the non-Twitter World, which stubbornly insists on continuing to need me.

Be so nice to someone today that you confuse him.

Passion is never out of fashion.

Pour your heart into whatever you do today. That's what hearts are for.

Engage your mind in whatever you do today. That's what minds are for.

Give a little love in whatever you do today. That's what love is for.

Share a little credit for whatever you do today. That's what credit's for.

Used wisdom here: Pre-owned insights. A patina of application is also available.

Being here, now and then, you get this amazing experience of almost channeling insights. Stuff just comes to you.

Twitter: The Collective Ouija Board of Wisdom.

Twitter: The Magic Eight Ball of Many Insights.

Wisdom at its best is a group endeavor. Virtue at its best is the same.

An intellect may sparkle and shine without ever touching wisdom.

Never confuse cleverness and wisdom, or obscurity and profundity.

Back in a bit! Keep the wisdom warm and the insights flowing!

Twitter is like the world's greatest cocktail party, and no one has to clean up afterward.

Healthy competition pushes us to push others to goad us all to be our best!

The best way to meet the future is with a plan in your mind, some hope in your heart, and a smile on your face.

Always honor authenticity, genuineness, and openness with a glad and outreaching heart.

You can tell what a culture values by what it pays for. Contrast entertainers and athletes with teachers and librarians.

Forgiveness is often an act of moral leadership.

Forgiveness can be an act of moral courage.

Aristotle said there are three kinds of friendships: Utility, Pleasure, and Complete. The third he also called Virtuous.

Utility friends give and receive benefits. Pleasure friends give and receive enjoyment. Complete friends give and receive all good things.

A good friend can be like a great book. And a great book can be like a good friend.

Masterfully written, well-made hardcover books give us works of art inside works of art!

I'm getting ready to have such a great day it may perplex and astonish me!

You be wise. And I'll be likewise.

Don't strive, don't jive, just come alive and thrive!

Apathy is a modern pandemic. So is confusion over what's really important.

Things turn out the worst for people who make the worst of the ways things turn out.

Late at night, my tweets begin to degenerate. They become Pre-Socratic.

My favorite Twitter people, or tweeps, are paradigms of renewable energy!

"Nothing really good and admirable is granted by the gods to men without some effort and application." Socrates (from Xenophon)

Self-discipline may be considered an art. It's something we can cultivate, grow in and get better at.

"Good company will edify you. Bad will rob you even of the wits you had." Theogonis in Xenophon's "Dinner Party"

Self-discipline, which looks easy for some, may be the most deeply cultivated in those who have struggled to master it.

"A philosopher's job is above all to learn." Socrates: again. We should all seek to be philosophers!

"Don't cry because it's over. Smile because it happened." Dr. Seuss

Twitter is one of the few addictions that can make us sharper and better!

I have to leave all you philosophers and philanthropists for a bit. But just like a good quote from Plato, I'll be back!

We are all cauldrons of potential.

We are all repositories of hope.

We are all authors of history.

We are the translators of the past into the future.

The most important thing I've learned from Socrates is the importance of relentless self-examination.

And to be careful what you drink.

Socrates insisted his fellow citizens examine their beliefs, attitudes, and behaviors. They insisted he drink poison and die.

General Life Lesson: Perplexity is usually a clue that something important is afoot. Don't shrug it off. Pursue your perplexity!

Little things add up. We live in a universe that seems to honor little things as they accumulate over time.

Twitter: Extemporaneous, improvisational group magic!

Always separate your wants and needs. I keep a shoebox for my needs, and rent a warehouse for my wants.

In the 1600s, Dom Perignon spent years trying to get the bubbles OUT of his wine. Moral: Take what you've got and Bubble On!

Great Design is Love – Truth, Beauty, Goodness, and Unity coming together.

Great design evokes head over heels infatuation!

Thursday is a good time to take stock of the week. Still time to do the undone, or undo the done!

Curiosity is one of the most important elements in a thriving company culture. Wonder. Interest. Active Attention. The Search.

Every major wisdom tradition focuses on what we pay attention to!

Someone tweeted: "You are perfect at your core." Thanks. It's the rest of the apple that could use some work!

I have a travel day coming up, and may not see you until very late. Keep up the great things going on.

Oh, the rigors of a day away from Tweeting!

I've got 24 hours of 140 space insights about life pent up in me and about to make my head explode. I had to come back and unload.

This moment is the doorway of infinite possibility.

I don't mean to get too mystical here! But it is fundamentally extraordinary how much is truly available to us.

It's important to ponder how much possibility is cut off for an individual caught in dire poverty and illiteracy.

It's equally important to try to do something about that.

I like to see you all getting philosophical, swimming in the deep end, and inviting others in as well! Get soaking wet with wisdom!

The rainforests may be among the best universities of life! Let's protect them well.

I'm off to go jog. You guys keep passing the ball of insight around, spinning it, and taking a shot now and then.

Two statements: one focusing, one freeing. Which speaks to you? 1. Everything matters. 2. Nothing is worth your worry.

I think of balance as a dynamic thing. We're usually off to one side or the other, but we can re-correct continually!

My glass on the table outside is already half full! And it's about to rain!

Paradox is always a sign that you're in the neighborhood of deep truth.

The distinction between emulation and impersonation is vital. Become like those you admire, but don't just ape the great.

There is a sense in which Pascal recommended an emulation of faith as an imitative habituation allowing the real thing.

Wisdom fills me, or else I'm just a bit bloated with hopefully helpful aphorisms from my extended time away!

So don't give me any static today for being far too epigrammatic this way!

I remember when I had so few followers here that I could communicate with more people by going into the yard and talking loud.

Character starts with what catches our attention, what we dwell on, and how we daydream. Attend carefully. Dream well.

Weeds grow fast, oak trees grow slow, but boy do they grow!

Imagine a square bicycle wheel. To improve it, you make it hexagonal, then octagonal. Then you realize it doesn't need more angles.

That's the learning curve.

Don't believe everything you hear, especially in the secret whispering of your own mind!

Twitter is my favorite place to go, partly because it's no trouble at all, but mostly because of all the great people here.

There is something to learn from every person you meet.

Week Six
Clarity, Love, Courage, and Play

Clarity is a sharp knife. Confusion is a dull blade.

Clarity is hard and powerful. Vagueness is easy and weak.

Clarity is active. Confusion is passive.

Clarity is the best quest of a badly crowded mind.

Clarity is the condition for wise choice – as rare as it is necessary.

Anyone care to fill in the blank? Money can't buy happiness, but: _____.

You can be unhappy in much greater comfort.

You can maybe get a long-term lease?

At least you can tip well any Maitre d' of Mirth!

That's just fine, because happiness is free, and it will make you richer in all the ways that count!

That last filling of the blank, you can take right to the bank.

Wisdom springs from unlikely sources. Keep your eyes open at all times!

Commercial pilots and great emergency room teams employ the simple tool of a checklist. It could benefit us all.

The checklist: Many simple things can be powerful when used well.

The checklist: So that distractions don't result in omissions.

The checklist: An itemized reminder of what not to neglect.

The checklist: Like any tool, it's only as good as it's designed to be. Craft yours well.

I'll be back in a few minutes. Please, continue tweeting among yourselves. No need to get up!

"Surprise is the greatest gift that life can give us." - Boris Pasternak

Even difficult surprises can deepen and strengthen us if we let them, and this ends up being a gift after all!

The great achievements of the past were the adventures of adventurers of the past. - Alfred North Whitehead

"When you relax, you can make miracles." - Tan Dun

"To forgive much makes the powerful more powerful."
- Publilius Syrus

A free act of forgiveness is in itself a liberation.

Noon: So far, so good! But of course, that's what the guy whose parachute wouldn't open said about half way down!

"Wisdom is to the soul what health is to the body." - La Rochefoucauld

"The strongest principle of growth lies in human choice."
- George Eliot (Mary Anne Evans)

Today is the day! Now is the time! Important new growth of the heart and mind await you!

The single greatest source of human motivation is the need to feel appreciated. William James.

I've never met so many great people as I have here in just a few weeks!

Twitter is the best surprise party ever! You can be the host, a celebrant, and the guest of honor all at once. And surprises never cease.

A Fantasy is a figment of the imagination; a Desire is an inclination of the appetites; a Goal is a commitment of the will!

Use your desires and fantasies to support your goals, not to substitute for them!

Fear can wake us up, or shut us down. Courage is necessary for all good things in life!

Got to run! When you guys finish up, someone turn out the lights. I'll be back tomorrow, looking for your fresh philosophical faces!

Someone just told me it's officially Love Day here on Twitter, and I should discuss the idea.

Love is the great connector, the ultimate support for unity, the engine of great accomplishments, and a deep source of joy!

Love is always a surprise – and inevitably a great one.

Love is Plato's Path to Good: The Superhighway of the Soul.

Love is the one dance of life that we're all invited to join.

Love is the great attractor, the master healer, and the main reason we're here!

Love is the ultimate safety rope for escaping Plato's Cave!

Sorry! I'm getting carried away. Which is always what happens with LOVE!

Love is the whirlwind of energy that can lift us all up to our dreams!

There's no rest in the love fest we now know as Twitter!

Love is the only source that can power us to our true purpose!

Ok, I'm running out of twisdom here: Love is Evol spelled backwards, an EvolUtion of the spirit!

When wisdom wanes, cleverness has to do a little of the heavy lifting! In service to love!

Whew! Good thing this wasn't Discuss Nuclear Fusion Day!

"Faith, Hope, and Love," my friends, "But the greatest of these: is Love"! – Paul the Apostle

"To love nothing is not to live; to love but feebly is to languish rather than live." - François Fénelon

"A loving heart is the truest wisdom." - Charles Dickens

Flowing insights to quench our thirst for communal wisdom: The Twitter Stream.

I remember my early days on Twitter, weeks ago, trying to figure out what to do, how to do it, and why I was even trying!

What started off frustrating ended up as the greatest, best party ever! A Twitter Lesson! Persevere! Don't give up!

We are all artisans crafting our lives.

"For to miss the joy is to miss all." - Robert Louis Stevenson

"Happiness lies in the fulfillment of the spirit through the body." - Cyril Connolly

We lift each other up each day.

On criticism: Lightning strikes the highest places!

"All fortune belongs to him who has a contented mind."
- Panchatantra

When I see a man anxious, I ask, "What does he want?" If he didn't want something not in his power, how could be anxious? Seneca

Seek to secure what endures.

Tweeting with the right people sharpens the mind and warms the heart!

"Explore thyself." - Thoreau

Retweet Joy: To take what sparks you, and pass it on to spark others! (The RT Joy Boy)

Retweet Joy: You can speak to others with what has spoken to you. Plus you get to give credit where credit's due!

As you are, so is your world.

Got to run take care of some philosophy business. Sagacity commerce. Profundity duties. Hold those thoughts till I'm back!

You guys are the superheroes of social media wisdom! The Justice League! The X-Men and X-Women!

We're overloading Twitter today! Twitter: Get More Capacity! We have RAPACITY for CAPACITY!

Alexander The Great: Hung out with Aristotle. Learned a lot.

Alexander's edge: He gathered information quickly, acted decisively, did the right not the easy, shared credit, and led from the front.

Philosophical Talent Available: Will Tweet for Crumbs of Insight.

Philosopher on Duty: Aphorisms Cheap! Epigrams customizable! Quotes available. Inquire assiduously.

I consider conversation among the ancients to be like a preliminary Beta test of what we're doing here. They got us rolling.

The unexamined life is not worth tweeting.

We reap what we sow! We can't assume that others will plant the flowers we want to enjoy!

We reap what we sow! So, sow so well, you won't be able to believe what you reap!

"It is neither wealth nor splendor, but tranquility and occupation, which give happiness." - Thomas Jefferson

"What is philosophy? Doesn't it just mean preparing to meet whatever will come our way?" - Epictetus

"The foolish man seeks happiness in the distance, the wise grows it under his feet." - J. Robert Oppenheimer

The courageous souls around us are here to remind us what we're here to be.

Only courage will crack the thick shell of possibility and yield us the treasures within.

Courage is willing to walk in darkness while shining a light for others to follow.

Courage is something we have deep down in us when we need it – if we'll just reach for it and act!

Courage is the power of choice even in the face of fear.

Ok, I'll quit riffing on courage now! Thanks, you all, for the fun of doing that together!

I wouldn't give four nickels for anyone else's paradigms.

What I bring to Twitter amidst its growing pains: Philosophy that works in pursuit of technology that works!

The Greeks considered pride a virtue, but Judeo Christian thought exalts humility, and is wary of pride.

Many draw a distinction now between proper pride and an improper sort of "pridefulness."

You guys have made some great points about pride! We can distinguish: pride in who you are and in what you've done.

Proper, or useful, pride-in-who-you-are is an appropriate measure of self-awareness and self-love.

Appropriate, or useful, pride-in-what-you've-done is a suitable satisfaction in your accomplishments.

Pridefulness is an inflated sense of self, diminishing to others, and capped by arrogance, often displayed in boastfulness.

But that's enough on pride. I'm thinking now about chocolate.

Wow! I've never had so many reactions to anything as to the word chocolate! Next Book: The Wisdom of Chocolate!

So much excitement from so many people! I am now the official philosopher of chocolatism!

Wonder, love, and play are the threads that should run from childhood through all our adult years.

Play is the source of creative leaps.

Play is one of the many things we need to relearn from children.

Play is the way Twitter works at its best.

Play is how work ought to feel, at least when it's done right.

Play is the key to great relationships.

Play is the joy of existence, a celebration of life.

Play is behind every great idea, every astonishing accomplishment, and every big dream ever dreamed.

Play may be the shortest path to a new friend.

Play is the dance of your soul.

The way play can lead to profound results is just another of life's great ironies.

How should we then live? Playfully. Wonderfully. Ethically.

Ethical Guides: The Publicity Test – Would I want this to appear in the newspaper?

Ethical Guides: The Moral Mentor Test – Would I want my most admired moral mentor to see me doing this?

Ethical Guides: The Mirror Test – If I do this, can I look at myself in the mirror and like what I see?

Ethics Guides: The Golden Rule Test – How would I want to be treated if I were on the other end of this situation?

Ethics is never a side issue; it's always a central issue.

Seneca said, "The best ideas belong to everyone." So thanks for all the retweets!

Nobody's perfect – but all my Twitter friends come pretty amazingly close!

To slightly emend Socrates, "As long as I live and breathe, I shall never cease to tweet philosophy."

We're the generation redefining age.

I'd like to redefine death as well, if we could – maybe into something more like a long afternoon nap in the Bahamas.

For the most part, we seem to feel like the age we deserve to be.

The only Fountain of Youth we have right now is one that springs forth from within!

For all its depredations and demands, there are many benefits of age.

Age is preparation!

Age is leverage!

Age is a good running start!

Age is acceleration!

Age is realism.

Age is the no-excuse-zone for common sense.

Age: Is it a blessing or a curse? It's often up to us.

I'm officially Heinz 57 today – an amalgam of all that I've experienced, thought, and done!

Fifty-seven years old! This is what sparked my reflections and tweets on age! Thanks for listening!

It's nice to be around for another birthday. Let's do many, many more! Now, I have to go be King of the Moment!

Evening: The embers of the day glow with images of what's been, and intimations of what's to come.

Evening: A time for gratitude, reflection, satisfaction, and just that touch of regret that's needed to inspire us tomorrow.

Evening: It's always a time to relax, recharge, and rethink – a time to plan and hope and love.

Evening: It sometimes takes the dark to throw new light on our hopes, dreams, and plans.

Evening: Time to celebrate the done, remember the undone, and prepare the yet-to-do.

Evening: Only when it's dark can you really see the immensity of it all.

Evening: The cool of the air evokes heat within and stirs new thoughts of what yet can be.

Evening: Time to put it all into perspective. No worries, no rush, just being. There is a relief that can lead to new life.

Someone has said she has four children under the age of eight.

Evenings with four under eight: Exhaustion beyond belief, and gladness beyond words. Astonishment when it all goes quiet. And love.

Everything that's worth doing matters. Nothing that's worth doing is easy. So commitment is always appropriate, and necessary.

Twitter: A black hole of time? Or: a party at The Mansion?

Twitter: Harvard Business School for LIFE. But lots more fun and no exams.

Twitter Encouragement Tag: "You're IT!" "No, YOU'RE it!" "You guys are so BOTH IT!" ... "Wait, we're ALL it!!!!"

Please go Google "Susan Boyle on Britain's Got Talent." It's an amazing video. And it's quite an event.

Then we can talk about it!

Susan Boyle: The picture of courage, immense self-possession, perfect centeredness, inner beauty, and a spirit of fun.

Susan Boyle: My definition of actualizing potential by allowing the energy of the universe to flow through you.

Susan Boyle: One small person amazing, inspiring, and energizing the world.

Susan Boyle: The Imponderable, Improbable, even Impossible Dream empowering us all to reach and achieve.

Susan Boyle: Her wondrous spirit washed over that hall in a flash, enveloping everyone, lifting them up and filling their hearts.

Susan Boyle: One moment. One person. One act of surrender to what's truly possible.

Susan Boyle: The power to change a face. The power to melt a heart. The power to cover the earth with belief. From one small village.

Susan Boyle: The immense, incalculable power of inner vision, humility, persistence, and play.

Susan Boyle: Our living lesson that when life provides a stage, sing your heart out and prepare to be blessed!

Two reminders of hope: Captain Sully lands a plane, and Susan Boyle takes off with a career – equally improbably, and both great.

Susan Boyle: A walking paradox, as are we all, so her example gives us hope.

On Susan Boyle, at first glance: "Things like to conceal their true nature." - Heraclitus

Susan Boyle: We're not too cynical and jaded to be touched by simple authenticity and genuine goodness when it sings.

Inside each of us is a bit of Susan. This is the stage of "Twitter's Got Talent." Now, it's time to take the stage! Simon will smile.

Who knew that the Socratic Simon Cowell would be the midwife of all this?

We're all like Clark Kent, or Peter Parker – somewhere deep inside, there's a superhero awaiting a need. Alert: The need is there!

Every now and then something comes to us like a cosmic wake-up call.

This has been a full and wonderful day, full of new discoveries and new vistas.

There is magic on Twitter! But it requires magicians like you!

Someone just said: "When you need motivation, motivate someone else!"

That contains a general principle with many applications.

When you need healing, heal someone else!

When you need loving, love someone else!

When you need forgiving, forgive someone else!

When you need encouraging, encourage someone else!

When you need to feel appreciation, show appreciation to someone else.

When you need help, help someone else!

Very often in life, what we give is what we get. Thank you for reminding me of this important truth.

When you need smacking, smack someone else? It would probably work, but I won't recommend it!

It's amazing the thoughts that percolate up here.

Communal wisdom is overflowing!

Wait! A cosmic realization! If you NEED chocolate, GIVE chocolate to someone else! My mailing address is available on request.

Every day, this is just the greatest party I've ever crashed.

Twitter-Crashers Unite! Eat the cake! Drink the bubbly! Dance to the band! It's the party that never ends!

I obviously like to mix it up here: From the perfectly platonic to the mildly moronic.

Insights are great. Living them is greater. We are all creating the future.

We range here from the mundane to the ethereal: On some days, simple reminders, on others, genuinely new thoughts.

This is a modern mix the academy never anticipated – more like Socrates on the street than a class in the college.

Your workspace is a dramatic arena. In it, everything counts. Everything matters.

Everything around you either conspires in favor of your goals or detracts from your pursuit of them.

If we could just strip away the pretense, we could live life to the full.

Authenticity and transparency allow great things to happen!

Sagacity and Silliness –
Philosophers and Priorities For Us All

You say I should sum up the great philosophers in six words each? Why didn't my professors think of this? Classes could have been so short!

Thanks for the challenge! Here they are in no particular order, as they come to mind, the big thinkers in six words each.

Plato: Know Thyself. Always follow the good.

Aristotle: Happiness is excellence in action daily.

Woody Allen: Darkness, death, and a cover charge.

Berkeley: To be is to be perceived.

Kant: We bring our categories to experience.

Hume: The only miracle is: We believe.

Ockham: Razor away complexities you don't need.

Descartes: Doubt is the beginning of certainty.

Hegel: Everything produces an opposite. Synthesis results.

Aquinas: The Five Ways show the Way.

Kierkegaard: Take a leap, and become yourself.

Wittgenstein: It's all about our language games.

Heraclitus: Everything changes, but character is destiny.

Feuerbach: You are what you eat daily.

Socrates: Hey, I'm asking the questions here!

Boethius: Philosophy consoles us in changing times.

Abelard: Under cloak of philosophy, we loved.

Pythagorus: You guys! I've got a theorem!

Emerson: Self-reliantly, think your own thoughts.

Thales: Everything is water – Help, I'm drowning! (Based on a story he once fell down a well while pondering the sky.)

Bacon: I like rigorous experimentation, and eggs.

Alfred North Whitehead: The greatest achievements come from adventures!

Camus: From the plague, Sisyphus, I rebel.

W.V.O. Quine: From a logical point of view.

Dewey: Educate for character, train for life.

Thoreau: Good thing Emerson owned a pond.

Epictetus: Liberate yourself from false, restricting beliefs!

Seneca: Set high goals – focus, believe, persist.

Lao Tsu: Follow the Tao with patient flow.

Confucius: Revere ancestors, join together, do good.

Marcus Aurelius: Meditate; co-create your fate; march on.

Machiavelli: Act quickly and use appearances well.

Hadrat 'Ali: Live your poem; depart with grace.

Augustine: Darkness can give way to light.

Nietzsche: Live out of your own resources.

Michael Scott: Buy my paper, live to regret. (If you don't watch The Office, you should.)

Dumbledore: It's all about choice, over talent.

Iris Murdoch: Paying attention creates your moral universe.

Can I add in some primary religious figures? I think I can!

Moses: Hang tough with Yahweh and prosper.

Jesus: Follow me and live fully forever.

Muhammed: Life is surrender and faithful obedience.

Zoroaster: There's good and there's bad: Choose.

Buddha: Now, stop tweeting and go live!

Someone just tweeted me that he can do all this in 5 words! So, for him, I have one more.

Adam Smith: Competition is the foundation, right?

Time to jog! Thanks for listening to early the morning musings. Now, you guys have a Twee H. D. in History of Philosophy!

New thoughts come when I get into the zone, where all the mind's clutter evaporates and a peaceful flow takes over!

You can learn a lot about yourself by noticing how you react to others.

I think paying attention is an art. We can get better at it with conscious practice.

The power of the will is easy to talk about, hard to use, and crucial for difficult times.

I believe in wisdom and silliness, in nearly equal measure. The Wisdom of Silliness should be a book.

Pascal understood the power of the will, when consciously applied. It's not easy, but profound, if done right.

Someone asked if I'm an elitist. I believe in excellence. But I love and value people regardless of whether they've attained it.

Harry Potter: Great lessons on love, courage, leadership, truth, ethics, friendship, happiness, and meaning!

I don't age on Twitter, or feel the effects of age. It's a little bit like a fountain of youth.

Sorry I haven't been around all day! Work! Even for a philosopher!

When the market goes down, I wake up and write!

There is a sense in which Emerson was our last public philosopher in the fullest capacity. I admire his reach.

The challenge with difficulty: When to resist, and when to release. Wisdom is the capacity to judge.

The challenge with exhaustion: When to resist, and when to release. Wisdom is the capacity to judge.

"Imagination is more important than knowledge." Einstein

Another one: "Where's my hairbrush?" Einstein.

My toes need some warm sand and cool breezes!

Investment king Jim Rogers, to his daughters: "Question everything, never follow the crowd, and beware of boys!"

The great people on Twitter are the ultimate worldwide support network!

Let's choose well, act wisely, and experience deeply today!

One of our friends on twitter has a job that requires her to go to parties all the time.

Why can't a philosopher's job involve lots of parties? Socrates managed to pull it off!

Whatever is worth doing is worth our full attention.

Wisdom Wednesday. Let's reflect on our priorities.

People first: projects second.

Impact first: income second.

Passion first: planning second.

Service first: self-interest second.

Conservation first: convenience second.

Reality first: appearance second.

Values first: choices second.

Asking first: telling second.

Listening first: responding second.

The good first: the pleasant second.

Aim first: action second.

Prepare first: propose second.

Attempt first: refine, second.

Truth first: preference second.

Children first: the rest of us second.

The inner first: the outer second.

Plato first: Aristotle second – Our ideals should guide our actions.

Love first: all else second.

I'm just sitting in a comfortable chair, zoned out for a few minutes to philosophize! It's fun sharing!

Live each moment with full awareness.

Make time today to take off your shoes and wiggle your toes, and just enjoy your digital freedom!

Some of the ancient philosophers would have LOVED twitter!

I hope I'm emulating what they would have done: observation blended with participation and cogitation!

Remember this today: Serious isn't the same as somber. Add a little silly to your life whenever you can!

If you dig deep, matter is more like mind, and mind more like matter, than we ever imagined. Both are stranger than we can think.

What seems safe is often most dangerous of all.

The path to excellence may be scary at times, but it's wide enough for the trip.

A twitter friend is stuck at a car dealership waiting on an oil change. Send her some clever tweets to entertain her! Oil try, too!

Changing the oil is a little like changing the baby – it has to be done but it's not much fun.

All of us who are a quart low ourselves should tweet her. What should we say? That de-Pennzoil whatever we're thinking!

We should do all we can with the Twitter WD 140. We just need to filter our thoughts well.

At least while she's not Mobil, she can read our tweets.

Someone tweets that he is very synthetic with your predicament.

I'm oddly bereft of good oil humor myself at the moment. I can usually get something going with grease.

You say you see the dealer? Tell him you're up for a little blackjack. It will help pass the time.

While you're there at the service department, why don't you get your tires checked – or striped, whichever you prefer.

If they ask to balance your wheels while you're there, say "Only if you can do it on your nose." And let us know.

In case they want to check your timing, remember to pause before the punch line.

I think we've done our job. That will be $148.76 for the lame humor, $432 for the warrantee, and $9 labor.

Some thoughts: as dusk turns to dark at mid-week.

Evening is upon us. Embers still glow in the ashes of the day. Tomorrow, use them to fire up new achievements!

The middle of the week is an exciting place to be. Many things have already happened. Many still hold great promise.

When you've used your mind, heart, and body through the day, you can rest content with the results, and prepare for a great tomorrow.

Every day, I try to live a prayer for the moment, and then one more for the morrow.

Tomorrow is nothing but open possibility. Choose or lose throughout the day!

There's a reason each of us is here. Part of it hinges on what we do tomorrow. So rest well, and arise strong.

The meaning of life isn't inscribed on a wall, or on a lost scroll in Tibet. Part of it is hidden away in each of our hearts.

In every human being, there is a small seed of philosophical wonder. Water it, nurture it, and watch it grow.

Each of us is the confluence of everything we've experienced. But we're also much more. When we come together, amazing things happen.

Every now and then I like to just relax and see what comes to me. Then I share.

Surprise someone with something good within the next 24 hours, and give yourself the great gift of that giving!

You Twitter friends are proof that we're here for each other, and to do great things.

Children have the sense of wonder that we all need to recapture and grow!

Passion provides possibility.

May this day be full of joy and goodness for you!

Love your Thursday! Still time to do what needs to be done, and undo what shouldn't have been done!

Dogs and philosophers do the greatest good and get the least reward. - Diogenes (who looked like a stray dog).

I just caught a glimpse of myself in the mirror, and I'm worried! Promise you're not just following me for my beauty, ok?

I couldn't even type that with a straight face. For one thing, it's a little too round.

Plato believed that justice starts at home, with proper inner harmony. Let's all make sure we're right within today!

Aristotle: Happiness is a life of excellence. Find out what that means for you, and enjoy living it each day.

Socrates: Only a life enhanced by self-examination can attain its full potential. Ponder yourself today!

A life that isn't dynamically balanced will never be properly full.

Anything worth doing is worth doing badly – at first, when nothing dramatic is at stake, and when you can still adapt.

Someone just said that feedback is the breakfast of champions. I like that.

Adaptation just may be the lunch of champions!

And what's the dinner of champions, you ask? The menu says: Big, plump, pan-roasted metaphors for explaining their success.

Self-knowledge is important in life. But how can we know ourselves? We're sometimes so elusive.

We're all masters of self-deception, so a measure of courageous inner looking should be augmented by: listening to others.

Just jogged! Deer flies appeared magically and tragically!
Ouch! Ouch! Lots of swats!

The years I walked, neighbors shouted Hi; now that I jog
they slow down their cars to cheer me on, and to see if I need
medical help.

Heraclitus (500 BC): Expect the unexpected!

Off for a quick early lunch snack! Keep up the love and
wisdom, tweet pack!

Knowledge without energy does nothing. Energy without
knowledge does wrong.

An old lady couldn't pay for her groceries. I said, "Put it
on my VISA." The whole store froze in time. The manager:
"God Bless You!"

I smiled all the way home.

The best thing that happened to me all week was the chance
to help someone in need. Keep your eyes open for your turn!

I even laughed out loud thinking about it later. It was such a
charge – so to speak!

Nothing will make you feel as good as helping someone who
needs it.

Or Lesson Number Two: If you're short of cash, get in front
of me in line.

The joy of a good deed is contagious. I couldn't buy something for the same money that would give me the same kick!

I really don't deserve so much satisfaction and glee from such a small thing, but that's the way life can work.

It was a tiny good deed, but an illustration that any good thing can travel far – especially through the feat of a tweet!

We should always be on the lookout for need of any kind and be ready to do what we can to meet it.

I knew that if I shared a reflection on my day's delight here, you guys would help me enjoy it even more!

It's said that to give is better than to receive. You can't give something good without receiving something better!

Opportunities can come disguised as almost anything! But they're all around! And they need us like we need them!

When we do good stuff and see the results, it's both humbling and ennobling, a paradoxical and wonderful experience.

Week Eight
Choice, Excellence, Listening, Comfort, and Confusion

Tomorrow's problems often come from today's decisions, so let's choose to decide well!

Choices are the little opportunities to craft our future each day.

The wild thing about choice is that we never know what events we may set in motion with even the smallest decision.

The significance of choice should not freeze us, but remind us of the drama within which we enact our small roles to great effect.

Choice always happens on the razor's edge of potential. We invite in one reality over another.

Another feature of choice is that it happens almost continuously, largely unconsciously, as an outflow of who we are.

The choices we notice and that give us pause are always opportunities for new clarity.

Some philosophies center on what we are. Others focus on what we choose. But we are what we become as we choose.

Choice is the voice through which we speak to the world.

Love energizes us, guides us, and blesses us every moment we allow it to!

With excellence: Don't hesitate – habituate!

An elderly relative died this weekend, and we spent a day going to his funeral. What was sad turned out well.

A funeral, then the cemetery: Two old soldiers presented an American flag to the elderly widow. They consoled and saluted her.

We went to a nearby house full of cousins who hugged and talked and caught up all afternoon. Merriment ensued.

Ladies who had played together as kids and teens saw each other for the first time in years, and remembered their past and laughed with joy.

It was a celebration of family, and of a time when relatives could form a friendship network of fun.

Some of the old ways that come from the old days should be preserved. We all ache for connection.

Is the clock your friend or foe? Find a way to make it work for you today. Let it be the metronome of your daylong dance.

Let's remember the infinite value of each person we meet today, despite any appearances to the contrary!

I like to start my day with a deep thankfulness for all you guys. The twitterverse is a new source of inspiration.

Bring a touch of the eternal fire to everything you do today! Life is meant to be a passion play!

We are artists of the possible, shapers of the actual.

Possibility is the raw material for all your creative work. Use it well!

Creation's not complete, unless you know what to delete!

Dip your toes into the cool water of new opportunities today! And when the water is right, jump on in!

Doubt is natural, but not always beneficial.

Belief is important, but not always right.

We dance with doubt each day. Choice can tame it if done right! But we're smart never to wipe it out!

Hope is the most essential nutrient of the soul, best absorbed from the light of right action.

I naturally extract the essence of each moment! And then I try to make the next one even better!

Squeeze every drop of juice from this day! Enjoy it deeply, and pass it on!

I always write from the heart and the head. Then, I hope for the best.

I haven't planned the day yet, so it's still pure potential. An open calendar is the greatest playground.

Take the potential of this day by the tail! Grab it! Embrace it! Use it well!

Is Wednesday a high hill or a low valley for you: The apex or nadir of the week?

I love Wednesday's high perch each week, from which we can survey what has been and what yet can be.

Give yourself time to ponder today. Working harder or faster won't help if you're not aligned with your top priorities.

We learn from difficulty.

When you witness real transformation, you can feel like you're in the midst of magic.

Let's make personal history today!

We come from hundreds of generations of adapters! If we'll just draw on that rich heritage, we'll prevail!

I can feel an Aristotelian Day coming on! Excellence as a habit! Happiness as virtuous action! And contemplation as the guide!

Passion is a sign of talent. Whatever moves your heart is a key to your proper path.

Passion is a sign of calling, a foretaste of excellence, a promise of positive impact.

Grip this day with passion!

May your day have a fun balance between the Apollonian (reason, order) and the Dionysian (passion, fun frenzy).

Keep this in mind in all things: Mediocrity is not an option! You are here for more!

If you see any sleepwalkers around you today, WAKE THEM UP to this time that will never come again!

We've been dropped into a world of high-speed challenge – there's no time to be average. Every day counts.

Excellence is etymologically "rising out from" – it can be talent rising from potential to actuality, or rising out of the crowd.

Never skip a day; skip THROUGH the day with child-like energy and fun!

Confucius says: The venerable ancestors from your past cheer you forth on your path.

This is the day. We are the people. The call is for us to answer. Let's do whatever good we can today!

Patience: If it's a virtue, it's not the same thing as procrastination or timidity. It's the strength to allow things their due time.

A great woodcarver has given me a perspective on patience: He talks about the necessity of listening to the grain.

The best carvers watch and listen to the grain. They partner with the wood. What's the grain of your situation right now?

Sometimes patience requires more strength and control than bold action.

Patience is a spiritual discipline that can yield great things.

The hardest things to learn are often the greatest things to use.

Patience can seem to be an old-fashioned virtue in a high-speed world. But it's now more important than ever.

Awareness precedes excellence.

Awareness is behind every masterpiece.

Awareness is leverage. Awareness is power.

Awareness, like patience, is an art, a skilled behavior we can cultivate.

The victor isn't always the one who acts fast, but the one who acts best. And that requires the timing that patience can give.

Any form of healthy control over difficult matters comes through effort and struggle.

Too often, we want to control the world around us without first controlling ourselves.

Control starts within. And then it moves out properly from deep inside that core.

The best form of control is guided by loving-kindness and a humble openness to learn.

We have two jobs: To make ourselves and to make our world into the best of which we're capable.

Imperfection doesn't require guilt, just more work!

Patience, Action, Awareness, and Love – all are vital for positive creation.

When we help others properly, we always help ourselves.

The master-apprentice model of education is so great, in part, because both parties learn and grow.

Just being around a master, you pick up things that can never be put into words.

An act for myself may strengthen me, but an act for another can strength us both, and the social fabric around us.

In the deepest sense, giving is growing, and free giving is also receiving.

The test of true giving, as distinct from being used: Is everyone better off as a result?

Do you give to live, or do you live to give?

I think I should explain the distinction.

Giving to live seeks to benefit the self. Living to give focuses outwardly and – paradoxically, done right – ultimately serves inwardly!

Service to others always most benefits the self that's doing the service.

Our world is shot through with wonderful paradox. To live without paradox is to live thin and flat.

May we all know when to act and, equally, when to wait.

May we all know when to serve, and when to allow others that same joy.

May we all know how to give with love, and also how to receive with grace.

May we all know when to do, and then when to leave undone.

May we all know when to work, and just as well, when to rest.

We all have the gift of experience. If we can be still and listen to our inner voice now and then, we can use this gift well.

Wisdom is one of our greatest renewable resources.

Wisdom is the energy and guide of virtue, and the only path to happiness.

Wisdom is the way of weaving the world into what it's intended to be.

For wisdom each day, sit quietly a while and allow life to speak.

Someone asked if there are any small ideas. There are ideas that seem small. But all rivers empty into the ocean.

Listening is one of the greatest gifts we can give another person. Really listening.

Deep listening requires more than concentration. It calls for a deliberate connection.

Listening in the fullest sense is a spiritual endeavor.

Attentive listening honors others. And it always elevates us.

Distractedness, by contrast, is disparaging.

Half listening diminishes others. And it always diminishes us.

Superficial listening most often isn't worth the time it takes. Like everything else that's crucial for life, great listening is an art.

Complete listening is a spiritual act.

Spiritual listening doesn't mean being uncritical. It isn't a lesser mode, but a greater one, incorporating all the others.

Deep listening is love in practice.

It's hard to be a good thinker without being a good listener. Socrates listened well.

Speaking without listening is like driving blindfolded.

When the connection is right, you can listen and hear with every fiber of your being.

True listening picks up more than words or even gestures can ever say. It operates on every level.

A great listener can understand respond well to every angle of what's being said.

Great listening is wholistic, and can involve more than one sense. You can listen with your eyes.

When we talk openly and listen fully, real magic can happen.

Complete listening always involves empathy. That means it's cognitive and emotional.

Two people in vibrant conversation, doing it right, are like great musicians jamming!

It would be immensely ironic for me to talk too much about listening. So I should cease. Thanks for ... LISTENING.

Comfort is like a rich dessert – fine and enjoyable to end a meal, but damaging as a constant diet.

Comfort is a great spa, but if you stay too long, a good prison.

There's nothing wrong with a little comfort to help you relax. It's always a fine servant, but a very bad master.

The main danger of comfort is its insidious charm.

Creative discomfort is the soul of a pioneer. A touch of discomfort can be good.

Comfort can nurture or it can smother. So always handle it well.

Comfort can recharge or it can restrain – it's always up to us.

Much in our world is confusing. But confusion itself need not be.

Confusion, like comfort, can be either good or bad.

A little confusion can be a good thing. It signals that something new is about to be born.

Confusion, used well, can stir up change.

Confusion is often a doorway of the possible.

Confusion, like comfort, should be used carefully and well.

Clarity is power, but clarity sometimes arises only from confusion.

When confusion occurs, embrace it and work through it. Very good things can result.

I woke up to thunder. The storm has passed, as storms always do. Life is filled with spectacular transience.

Light is breaking, as it always does. Life is filled with new beginnings.

I just fed a red Cardinal who shook off the storm and got down to business for the brand new day.

The louder the thunder, the more cleansing the storm: Or at least, so it seems to me.

Every moment offers a new start.

Thunder has been replaced with bird songs. And such is the way of life!

Nature will teach us daily if we look, listen, and think.

The bolts of lightning brilliant and fast can startle us awake, like creative new ideas.

We speak of a creative flash, or a thunderbolt of insight, for good reason. But without our action, it's just light and sound.

Storms can clear the air in nature and in life.

A catharsis is a cleansing emotional storm full of sound and fury that can signify something great.

When you give yourself a few minutes just to sit and enjoy some calm, amazing thoughts can arise in your mind.

I try to give myself this gift each day: A few minutes to listen to any lessons my unconscious might have for me to learn.

Someone wants one piece of advice on writing. What's my number one tip?

Just let yourself write, knowing you'll rewrite. Pile up raw materials at first with minimal editing. Simply flow. Craft it later.

Signs of the unconscious: A thought that integrates lessons over time, one that's non-deliberative and intuitive rather than reasoned.

One more mark of the unconscious at work in writing: A sense of passive reception – with genuine surprise and delight.

I don't necessarily think of the unconscious mind as superior to the conscious mind – just different. We need both.

"I am multitudes." But, I'm on a good program of diet and exercise, so please don't worry about me at all!

Western patterns of thought have been attenuated since the "Enlightenment" with its emphasis on the senses we understand.

The Western focus is on testing appearances for truth – the Eastern is on getting behind appearances for the truth.

A question was just raised as to where to get real insight, from experts or cab drivers!

Experts are like witnesses, all over the spectrum from clear to clueless. Each has a bias. We consult, and then we decide.

Cab drivers may be less invested than experts but they're typically more passionate, and may talk to more people!

I was once asked where the philosophers are now. I said many are the town car and limo drivers of America.

Drivers see funerals, weddings, Girls' Night Out, and busy business people. They talk and listen and think.

They witness human nature at its best and worst, and often for extended periods. Then they have time to mull it all over.

They provide this lesson: Paying attention to what we see, and processing what we experience can pave a road right to wisdom. Drive it home!

When you see anger, think first: Unhappiness.

When you see anger, feel first: Compassion.

Unhappy people aren't always angry, and angry people aren't always basically unhappy, but the two often pair.

Love is the great alchemy of life.

When abstract philosophers soar, the rest of us tend to snore.

Remember The 7 Cs of Success: Conception, Confidence, Concentration, Consistency, Commitment, Character, and a Capacity to Enjoy.

That's the most completely universal framework for success in anything we do!

What of Communication, Creativity, or Collaboration? All are applications in particular circumstances of one of the other Cs!

Encourage wonder where you see it. Dwell in it when you feel it.

We could have lived our whole lives without finding each other. Savor your Twitter friends every day!

We come together for brief moments and plant seeds for all time.

The Twitter Imperative: Give and receive. Do and allow. Touch and be moved. Share what you can.

It's wondrous, and scary, and gratifying to think of the gifts we would have missed without Twitter!

I look at your photos lining my screen, and some beautifully designed avatars as well, and feel glad and thankful for you all!

"That man is the happiest who has the most interesting things to think about." Timothy Dwight

Good morning! The day is full of possibility, and we all have front row seats – then we get to be on stage!

I just spoke in Boston. No one could find my great custom-made slides. No problem. We rocked the house without them.

When things go wrong, just adapt! Breathe deep, smile big, and bring confidence! It works!

When things go nuts, don't go crazy – go creative, big-time, instead!

When chaos descends all around, those who stay calm, think well, and act fast can prevail.

When things fall apart, work your magic. People will see it and appreciate you more.

When everything around comes unglued, just ramp it up, amp it up, and vamp it up! And enjoy to the max what results!

Excellence can overcome almost anything you face.

When you know what you do, inside and out, you can improvise the greatest jazz any time it's needed.

Structure and freedom, the old and the new, tradition and creation make the future together.

I always have 1-3 backup plans. When they run out, I just jump in – and that's when the real magic happens.

Hope for the best, prepare for the worst, and always be willing to go all out.

Boston is now vibrating with the wisdom of the past, the paths of the present, and the promise of tomorrow.

The sword of the spirit can cut through any knot.

Before any presentation I always ask: "How can I love these people today?"

Love conquers all.

Work can be a joy, a dance, a celebration – never old, and always new, if it's fueled by passion each step.

Pour your heart into whatever you do. Why should you ever settle for anything less?

Work that's well done can bring thankful bliss!

Every day, positioned right, we can feel new wind in our sails, and at our backs. We can glimpse new horizons that await us.

When our passion wanes, we need a new start – a new beginning to spur us on.

Here on Twitter we have backstage passes to the great concert of life.

My flight's canceled! All backups are full! I got creative, jumped airlines and paid $1,000 extra for a last seat, row 20. Still smiling!

The more lemons life hands you, the more lemonade you can make. And, at a certain point, you just have to spike it!

We need to laugh whenever we can at the absurdities life sometimes throws us.

Hey, I have the ultimate edge – I have friends in TWIT Places!

I don't see anyone else stuck in this airport surrounded by Twitter friends! You guys help make it work!

We just have to roll with the punches – tropical fruit punch, and all.

Even the Stoics would have to go into the lotus position here at Logan, chant a bit, and maybe hum.

I've got the chant down: Ommm gonna save money and buy my own plane. Ommm gonna take up a Twitter collection ... Ommm.

Someone just asked me about "sitting up front" on the plane.

I've only had the jump seat in private jets. Once a pilot let me fly in a snowstorm! Right seat. Co-pilot.

First officer Tom: "Good morning Ladies and Twittermen. We're now number one. Fasten your tweetbelts and prepare for tweet-off!"

Ok, I'd better actually go get on the plane so they can have some fun onboard.

"The most wasted of all days is one without laughter." ee cummings

I'm the custodian of my cognitive and emotive capacities, and I'm cleaning up today!

"Things are only impossible until they're not." Jean-Luc Picard

Despite all my air travel problems of late, I really appreciate the people of the airlines, and especially those on the front lines.

The airline industry deals with the general public and weather – two of the most unpredictable forces in the world.

The adventure of the week was wild, chaotic, and fun!

Silence, The Sea, Uncertainty, Work, and Logic

We flow and gush here with words, and wisdom, and wonder!

I like metaphors from the old days. Newer ones just often don't have the same zing.

Compare: "The pen is mightier than the sword." "The laptop is mightier than the Glock 9." Just not the same ring.

The old organic, pastoral, and craftsman metaphors were great. Many modern analogues tend to fall flat.

My brain after a travel day is not at 100%. Running about 50% of the neural capacity today, max.

"I will permit no man to narrow and degrade my soul by making me hate him." Booker T. Washington

I like to think of Twitter as a wonderful, self-selected community of sages and lunatics.

I thought about posting a close up, front on photo as my Twitter avatar, but chose something more oblique instead.

Too much of me is not a good thing.

It'd be like when I once spoke on Beauty to three thousand plastic surgeons and some later sent me estimates!

At the end of the last century, it was all about great abs. Now, thanks to Twitter, it's all about great avs.

Ok, I have to go solve some of the mysteries of the world beyond the bounds of Twitter for about an hour or so. Back later!

It's Mother's Day!

Mothers! Happy day! Dads: Don't worry! Everyone burns toast now and then! After you drop the egg, crack a joke too, and all's fine!

Fathers, Sons, Brothers: This is a day to show you care about those who care every day! Honor the mom in your life!

On Twitter, friendly concern, compassion, insight, and a clever sense of fun rule. Put them together, and you hit Twitter gold.

"Life is a moderately good play with a badly written third act." Truman Capote. I would add that the casting is incredible!

Age gives us raw materials and opportunities for philosophy and wisdom, but it can guarantee neither. They're up to us!

We all need wisdom, and it can be hard to get. Some are just not up for the fight. But there's joy in the end when you persist.

Twitter: A surprising proof that a community of souls can form without any face-to-face physical presence.

"We become aware of the void as we fill it." Antonio Porchia (Profundity Alert!)

I'll try to do something or say something at least semi-profound today!

Many have told me that, when laid off from work, they felt set free. Life's unexpected adventures are sometimes great.

Philosophy is like music: many kinds, many styles.

Some philosophy, like some music, may not be right for you. When you find your proper style, you can grow with the flow and be wise.

Philosophy can lift you up, or calm you down, cause you to ponder, or make you dance.

Philosophy comes from pure wonder, proceeds through real effort, works with reason, and can reach the heart and mind.

In its aphoristic form, philosophy is insight set to the music of the spirit.

Somewhere in the space between poetry and prose, epigrammatic philosophy lives on.

Philosophy as theory can make you think hard. Philosophy as practice can help you live well.

Philosophy done badly can make you hate thought. Philosophy done well can enhance all you think.

Philosophy isn't an option. Learn to do it well or you'll likely do it wrong.

Philosophy is an activity, never inert knowledge. Let's get wisely active today in what we think, do, and say!

I'm a philosopher, but then so are you. I just admit it and get paid for it!

Encourage outstanding performance! Treasure quality when you find it! Nurture goodness all around you!

Always bring more than you expect. Never expect more than you bring. That is the transformative approach. Alchemy results!

Wit Happens.

Bring a spark of fun to something or someone today, and you'll do a good deed that will lift YOU up!

3D Success: Discover your talents. Develop those talents. Deploy them into the world for others as well as yourself!

Truth is your friend, and a better foil than foe.

Socrates believed we sharpen ourselves by getting beyond our own heads through contact with each other.

Be a detective today, a chief investigator of possibility. Don't let false clues get you off the path.

Treat every person you meet as if they are the most important soul in the world!

This moment will never exist again. Stretch it.

This moment will never exist again. Fill it.

This moment will never exist again. Use it well.

This moment will never exist again. Share it with love.

Your investments go up and down. Your projects wax and wane. But your moments of time will be what they are forever. Relish them.

Someone just said: "Beautiful." I have to reply. But first I want to say thanks.

Beautiful: This world is, this life is, and if we do it right in our thoughts and our actions, we can be too.

There's no pressure when you learn to live and breathe in the moment. You become immediate in all the right ways.

No one can dictate how you embrace this moment, how you use it, and send it off full of what only you can bring.

Someone asks: Is Shakespeare a philosopher?

Shakespeare is a philosopher! And a poet! And a prophet! And a lover! As should we all seek to be!

The flow of time can carry us along to the ultimate place we belong, but only when we listen and act with discipline and courage and love.

What is the role in your life of quiet? What is the role of noise?

Quiet helps me think. Quiet lets me relax. Quiet centers me so I can open up to insights bubbling deep.

Quiet is something I need each day. Too little is tough. Too much is hard. Just enough can be magical.

Quiet is rare and as valuable as anything so hard to acquire.

We sometimes fear quiet and fill the time it could be ours with noise of our own, a defensive din to keep thoughts and feelings away.

The sounds of nature are unlike man made noise. There is music in a rain forest that allows quiet to reign.

Serendipity. When we're quiet, we can listen for those small inklings that are doors to great things.

I am a talker. I am a thinker. I play guitar. I can be loud. But I need a little quiet more than anything else.

When it's quiet enough, you can hear with your whole body and soul.

If you've ever had a day of silence, you begin to wonder what your voice will sound like when you eventually hear it again.

Silence is a dangerous and wonderful undertow that can sweep us out to the depths of new understanding.

Too often we struggle and shout for help when we should be floating with the silence to where it would take us.

Even when playing a guitar, I can catch a moment of silence before I bend that next note. Learn to notice small things.

Silence is the great beer, a true cosmic brew. Our noise is just the foam on top.

Power comes from the silence beyond and learning to channel it well.

In space, silence and light are found piercing the dark in their own different ways. In life they work together, too.

The silent still point within can withstand the loudest storm without.

There is no way to understand quiet than to be quiet. There is no way to understand good than to be good. Being precedes seeing.

We don't always need long stretches of silence. We don't always need big meals. Sometimes a snack does the job.

Great music is not the opposite of silence. Each celebrates the other.

The human voice can be the most beautiful embodiment of sound, or at other times the worst.

A human whisper can be the most mysterious sound, and the loveliest, or the most heinous.

Sometimes I get the best out of Twitter when I sit as quietly as I can and let the words of others enter me and work.

Ponder quietly, with an open heart, and new ideas can arise.

From even a short time of rich, dense silence, philosophy can ensue.

I live very near the ocean. It acts on me in many ways.

The ocean: An endless horizon, evoking the infinite, expressing our aspirations for limitless domains.

The ocean: Like us, mostly salt water – the ancient source, and affinity of life.

The ocean: Always the same, and always changing, just like the life that surrounds us.

The ocean: The waves and spray, the storms and calm, the sparkle of the sun, and the hurricanes of change.

The ocean: A symbol of new things, hidden treasure, and the adventures that yet await us. Danger and promise – like each new day.

I live by the ocean so I can walk on the sand and contemplate the beauty that can lure us forth.

Philosophy begins at the edge of the sea. Philosophy happens in sight of the water.

The sand on the shore: How many grains? The tide comes and it goes, but these grains endure.

I take off my shoes to feel the warm sand, and walk in the water to think, with nothing particular in mind. And yet, ideas emerge.

Wrightsville Beach, near my house: A sacred, healing place – a special location of insights and dreams.

A seven-mile beach, maybe eight, that draws me in when I need it, and gives me dolphins as companions in thought.

It's so healing and inspiring. And I have it every day, when I'm not traveling to give others the benefits it provides to me.

The ocean relaxes and inspires me. That order of effect is important.

The sea reminds me of how small I am and how powerful – two equally vital truths.

This is the first place I've lived where the sky at night is dense with bright stars glittering from afar and calling me to dream.

Have you ever noticed that on cloudy, rainy days, the colors of the grass, trees, and flowers are so much more intense? They can glow.

I like that as a metaphor for us.

The rain continues to bring out the garden's glow.

Flower power in a shower: Must be glad, can't be dour. Go forth then and bloom!

Do you talk to express, or to bless? There's a huge difference between the two.

Some seem to talk mainly to impress.

To express or impress is all about me. To bless is mainly about you.

Someone asked whether memory is the mother of all wisdom.

It seems true: Without memory, we just skate on the thin ice of an eternal present, learning nothing, having no guide.

If memory is indeed the mother of all wisdom, mistake may be its father.

Watching some people think is like seeing hot dogs made. Watching others is like witnessing a master chef.

Each life is a story, the first chapters written by others – then it's co-authored, and as it builds, we can take more creative charge.

Write your story well.

Your story isn't you, but a great part of you. You transcend the past and can overcome the present, if you use your story well.

We love other's stories so because we live narratives of our own, and always seek hints for how things can turn out.

From the oral tales of old, through scriptures, poems, novels, and films, we shape our inner selves in response to what we envision.

The questions we can't agree on include life, death, freedom, God, good and evil, and meaning or cosmic purpose.

Existentially central questions allow of no real proof. You take a leap regardless of your reaction, and that leap shapes your life.

So many of the most important things in our lives unfold under the fog of uncertainty.

Why is there so much uncertainty in life? Perhaps it's needed to force us to grow.

We all want answers. But a glut of information might stunt our development. Having all the answers could cause spiritual atrophy.

Uncertainty may be necessary for many of the best things we experience.

Uncertainly can serve us, if it goads us on to the new.

Celebrate uncertainty now and then!

A fear of uncertainty is one thing that makes humble openness so hard.

Too many of us prefer a false certainty to the vulnerability of openness.

That's what makes for prejudice, dogmatism, and intellectual arrogance. And, ironically, it encourages timidity.

Not even the wise Greeks sufficiently appreciated the virtue of humility. But they did condemn hubris, or wildly excessive pride.

Someone has asked this question: How can we flourish and not flounder in the face of uncertainty?

There is an irony about uncertainty. When we're very young we deal with it a lot. And we're fine. But we begin to seek certainties.

The more certainties we seek, and the more we think we have, the more unsettled we become when uncertainty appears.

Flourishing instead of floundering depends on inner attitude and cultivated skill.

We can't deal with uncertainty like artists without the benefit of abundant practice. It's a skilled behavior arising from within.

Consider the possibility that uncertainty is a gift.

Occupation and vocation: What you do to live and what you live to do.

Occupation and vocation: Labor and love.

If your occupation and vocation are compatible, you're really very lucky. If they're simply the same, you're truly blessed.

Your occupation need not define you. Your vocation shows who you are.

We all need balance in our lives.

Balance is a dynamic and ever-changing thing. It's like a tightrope walker, who is always correcting in little ways.

We all have to balance what we want to do and what we have to do.

Sometimes we get to do what we love. Sometimes we get to love what we do. Sometimes we're provided for, and sometimes we provide.

The real secret in life is taking what's necessary and making it desired.

If we can love to do what we have to do, we can do all things well.

The closer together we can bring desire and duty, the better off we are.

When you can get paid from following your calling, you've hit a real jackpot in the casino of life.

When love and work fill your soul with no competition or strife, you're already living in a part of heaven.

We can't overstate the importance of being present in the moment while going about our day. Unease happens when we stray from the now.

Being present is a practice requiring practice! And like everything important, it pays off.

The silent point of presentness is so small yet so expansive. We are a powerful paradox, and so is all our life.

Our sense of calling can be subtle or strong, but it's always important for what we can be.

We're here for a journey together, an adventure of peril and promise. The deepest values can guide us well.

We're never just doing – we're always becoming.

I had a few thoughts on hope during my daily jog just now.

Hope is never drowned under a sea of troubles. It's never soaked heavy and wet by the storm rains. Hope is buoyant. Hope floats.

Hope isn't knowledge or belief. It's not expectation at all, but a positive embrace of the future – a deep longing for good that's affirmed.

Hope is a form of trust.

Active optimists whip the world into shape. Active pessimists seek shelter.

Choose to be what's best.

A friend wanted me to reflect on logic today. I don't see him around, but since I travel soon, I'll get right on it.

Our word 'Logic' comes from the Greek word 'Logos,' which meant philosophically the structure or rationality of the world.

The logic of anything is its structure, whatever makes it work. For example, there is a logic to metaphor.

More strictly speaking, logic is the formal structure of thought and the world that allows us to reason in a truth-preserving way.

Do I hear a yawn? Hang in there a little more! This will all pay off.

When we follow the laws of logic, we guarantee in our reasoning that if we've started with truth, we'll end up with truth.

In ordinary language, however, we get sloppy with the word – for example, we use "That's logical" to mean, "That makes sense."

When people say "But the world isn't logical!" They often mean, "It doesn't make sense!" or "You can never know what's next."

Sometimes, they mean that there is much more to life than just logic, and of course, in this, they're right.

When philosophers say that reality is formally structured by logic, they don't mean we can make full sense of why things are.

And they don't mean that logic is the most important thing about our world.

"Logic structures reality" just means that, by using logical thought, we can reason well from truth we see to other connected truth.

Logic allows us to follow the threads of truth, the breadcrumbs of reality that mark the path to expanded knowledge.

The laws of logic themselves tell us nothing about facts of the world, but only about the structures that support good reasoning.

If A is x, then A is not non-x. Nothing can both have and not have the same quality in the same respect at the same time.

When you are given the truth of "If P, then Q" and know the truth of "P" the truth of "Q" will follow.

Or, to reverse this, when "Q" follows from "P" and you know "Q" is false, you can reliably infer "P" to be false as well.

I've just illustrated the laws of logic with the principles of Non-contradiction, Modus Ponens, and Modus Tollens.

But don't worry: there won't be a test.

In trying to grasp complexity, we have to guard against fallacious reasoning – or a failure in logic.

Many fallacies are obvious, yet some are quite subtle. Others are almost impossible to spot. But they can deflect us from truth.

This ends the professorial discourse on logic – fortunately, or I'd lose most of my followers here! And, quite logically!

Now we need to get practical in our take on logic. There's useful wisdom here.

We're too easily content with the first thoughts we have. Logic helps us dig deeper.

Many people treat thought and talk as forms of expression, not as roads to truth. Logic is about getting at truth.

Reason is perception, intuition, memory, and logic working all together.

Language is a link to a landscape greater than our smallest selves. Logic strengthens that link.

When you abandon logic and walk away, you relinquish your grip on the truth.

Logic isn't our prime contact with truth, but the way we best process and explore it.

Logic alone can't create a life or lift up a soul. But without it, we're always lost.

Logic is a light on our path, and never the path itself.

Logic and love must unite. Neither is complete alone.

Logic without love is cold. Love without logic is blind.

Logic can't give us a leaping flame, but neither can it extinguish one that burns bright.

Logic will serve us well, but only if we use it right.

Logic is a tool of discovery – nothing more, and nothing less.

There's formal logic, informal logic, inductive logic, lateral logic, conceptual logic, and fuzzy logic that gets on my pants.

The logic of blogs we can call Blogic.

The logic of clogged drains: Clogic?

The formal structure of being stodgy: Stodgic?

Logically, I should have stopped while I was ahead – if indeed I ever was.

Confidence, Simplicity, Elegance, And Service, With Flow

Truth is as infinite as reality. Most truths we deal with are finite. But they eventually all connect up.

Wisdom is a bit like a subset of knowledge – it's knowledge about how to live well – and it's supposed to be embodied.

I've been asked: What's our main contact with the truth? The answer is really simple.

Our discerning minds: Our senses are our primary contacts with appearances. But only our minds can penetrate to truth.

The senses and intuition provide raw materials. The reasoning and discerning mind has to judge them all.

The mind organizes and interprets and sifts through possibility to put us in touch with the world. And that touch of contact is truth.

Wondering, pondering, thinking, musing – over the second cup of coffee.

Just got a phone call. I'm needed in the hotel ballroom for the famous "Sound check." Will they take my check, or should I bring cash?

Testing One Two Three. Can you guys hear me? Is this ON? Tap, Tap, Tap. See? I know all the real insider professional speaker stuff!

Speaking can be pure joy. It can be a form of love.

Everything we do should result from love.

Never open a business unless you love people and want to serve them. Any other motive will eventually come undone.

Keep the wisdom flowing.

Back Home from speaking! What a day! I had a great time with a group this morning in Naples! Then a car and two planes!

A day to wipe out a philosopher. But I have you guys. Plato had his Toga. I have my Twitter. Each is as breezy as the other.

I'm utterly worn out. But in a good way! Getting ready to plop down and snooze. I now dream in tweets.

Always remember while I'm gone: It's not just Socrates or Aristotle – you need your very own Plato-mvmorris!

Welcome to a day that's unique, a day that's never existed before and that never will again! Embrace it! Fill it with your best!

I just fed the birds, and I love watching them a few feet away get their own start on the day.

The birds are songs on wings. So should we be today.

Find a breeze this morning to lift you up. Then soar on to your proper heights.

We see such a small spectrum of the world's radiant energy. We live in a Great Expanse, bathed in power and in hope.

Everything is more wonderful than it seems.

Everything is more mysterious than it seems.

Everything is more magical than it seems.

Everything is deeper than it seems.

Everything is more potentially revelatory than it seems.

If we open ourselves to learn more of these things, we can.

Anything around us can be a peephole to the infinite. We should take care to look closely and be prepared for surprise.

Cast your glance wide and deep. Wonder can result.

When I close my eyes, the light doesn't vanish. It's up to me to see what's here. I'll keep the eyes of my heart wide open today.

My trip was amazing. The audiences were great. I love to make waves with ideas and watch people surf them well!

Plunge in to the wild water of the day and paddle out to catch your perfect wave!

When the thinker is ready, the thought will appear!

Plato and Aristotle? Pass the champagne bottle. The French know what to do, to counteract Camus.

I had some random thoughts on my 90-minute walk in edge of the water that I think I'll share. Nothing earth shaking, but nice to remember.

This is a world of pain and joy, sadness and gladness, limits and freedom, ease and difficulty. Never be too surprised.

Enjoy what can be enjoyed, endure what can be endured, learn what can be learned, and you'll be what you can be.

Ideals are to guide and inspire us, not to accuse and discourage us.

The discipline to be what we can must be paired with the ability to enjoy what we are.

A life of all ease, or no ease at all, would prevent the best sort of growth.

The things that challenge us the most can also deepen us the most, depending on what we bring to them.

Another beach revelation: The endless varieties of the human form are lessons unto themselves.

Getting whatever you want is a poor prescription for life. We need first to learn to want what we truly need.

Thirty birds flying in close formation, turning, landing, in perfect unison: This is a lesson for us all.

Almost anything can eventually spark insights if you let it work in your heart and mind.

I believe we're here to become something great. And learning from each other is important for the process.

I love bringing new ideas, or new thoughts about old ideas, to you all here. When I see your reactions, it helps me dig deeper.

Someone asked a couple of days ago to reflect a bit on confidence. I finally have time and will do so now – confidently, of course.

Confidence is a facilitating condition for success in almost anything we do.

You can succeed in some things without much confidence – you can be surprised by success – but it can be an important help.

Confidence isn't arrogance, or presumptuousness, or overweening pride. You can be humbly confident in what you do.

Confidence isn't a predictive belief either, a conviction that you will succeed in some endeavor and get the outcome you intend.

Confidence is an attitude of positive expectation that directs the mind and generates action.

When confidence intersects with belief, it's more a belief-in than a simple belief-that.

Confidence causes us to form certain thoughts rather than others, and to notice some things more than others.

Confidence launches action. And confidence allows for patience.

Confidence, properly grounded, inspires.

We distinguish beliefs, emotions, and attitudes. A belief is a conviction. An emotion is a feeling. An attitude is an orientation.

Racism is an attitude that results from beliefs, feelings, and actions. It then itself generates beliefs, feelings, and actions.

Optimism is an attitude that results from beliefs, feelings, and actions. It also then generates beliefs, feelings, and actions.

If you want a new attitude, seek to entertain the beliefs, experience the feelings, and perform the actions that attitude would suggest.

If you want to lose an attitude, seek to entertain the beliefs, experience the feelings, and perform the actions its contrary would suggest.

To become confident, act like you're confident. To act this way convincingly, first know your stuff.

Most of all, remember this: The best confidence arises from the best competence and command.

Competence alone can't guarantee confidence. You can be good without feeling it. Confidence is an extra step and it's always up to you.

An attitude isn't said to be true or false, but reasonable or unreasonable, justified or unjustified, helpful or unhelpful.

Unreasonable, unjustified confidence is rarely helpful at all.

Reasonable, justified confidence is helpful and powerful any time.

We can grow or erode our confidence by how we act and think.

When you become a master of controlling your thoughts and feelings, you can become a master with your attitudes, too.

Courage is a virtue, always good to have. Confidence isn't a virtue, but an attitude that's great to have, when justified.

To see the absurdity of unwarranted confidence, watch reality television competitions and listen to the braggarts talk.

They make two mistakes: They've not yet produced the realities the confidence ought to reflect. And they confuse confidence with arrogance.

Good confidence can be cultivated. And it can help us prevail.

Sometimes on Twitter, there is a crystalline flame of insight that slows down time, and speeds up the mind.

I love it when we get talking about some topic that can perplex us. It's like we all bring our little flashlights into the dark.

I look through the darkness and see this light and that one, and another over there. Each question and comment brings illumination.

I'm drawn to your light, as you may be to mine. We begin to converge, and suddenly, we can see a lot more together than we ever saw alone.

A friend just asked through email about elegance and simplicity.

In science, an elegant theory is one that does great work from the resource of a beautiful simplicity.

In modern fashion history, consider Grace Kelly and Cary Grant. Elegance is rooted in appropriate simplicity.

Less is more, within the bounds of good style and our over-arching intent.

Elegance never shouts. It whispers with power.

Simplicity and elegance require confidence. When we're unsure, we complicate things.

Undue complexity always bespeaks a lack of command, and a corresponding lack of self-confidence.

The best simplicity requires mastery, and can display it beautifully.

The best philosophy is elegant and simple, not complex, convoluted, and obscure.

Our work should manifest the mastery that produces elegant simplicity.

Work from the heart is simple and pure.

Work that flows from love can be elegant in every way.

In life, we move from simplicity to complexity, and, when we do it right, on to the greater and deeper simplicity that can then emerge.

The wonders of elegance never cease to amaze those who can see and understand.

Create, then edit. Do both with your whole heart, and elegance can result.

Simplicity is not a complicated thing, but it can be as hard as anything equally great.

Elegance seduces by enthralling our hearts.

Complexity can hinder and constrain us. Masterful simplicity invites us forth.

Complexity may be a journey, but it's never the destination. Simplicity is the goal that alone can justify it.

Undue complexity confounds. Well-earned simplicity invites.

Those who master are clear. Those who don't know thoroughly cannot explain simply.

We should never shirk the responsibility to understand complexity, but we don't really get it until we've reached the simplicity beyond.

The simplicity that hasn't struggled with complexity is fit for our youth, but maturity requires simplicity to be earned.

I enjoy and sometimes relish complexity on the trail of truth. But I never rest content short of the unified simplicities below.

Elegance is as rare as it is wonderful. Aspire to it in all things.

Simplicity is context dependent, has many contours, and is often hard to define, but the more we know, the better we recognize it.

Wisdom is all about simplicity and elegance. The most practical truths are rarely convoluted.

Many things block us from the best traits we should have. Sometimes the most we can do is struggle nobly.

Nature is our best school, if we know how best to learn from it.

I'm sleepy too early, drowsy too soon. Nodding prematurely. Zoned out too quick. The wild run of the day had soporific punch.

Finally I am going to tear myself away from this ongoing feast of insight, kindness, silliness, and knowledge. Good night my tweeps!

Daybreak! The delicious first rays of the sun are calling us forth!

The surf's up already! Is your board in the water yet? Let's see some tricks out there!

The road of the day is open and straight! Ladies, and Gentlemen: Start your engines!

The sky is blue, the grass is glowing in the slant of the early sun, and some puffy white clouds float by.

The beach is beckoning me on to some salt-water philosophy.

Someone mentioned passion for life and for our work.

The concept of passion: Does your soul leap, and do your molecules dance? Do you fly without effort? That's passion!

Passion catches you up in the moment, and stretches the moment itself! Time stands still to salute.

The greatest passion comes from beyond us, fills us, and lifts us up!

Then it draws others to us, when it's used well. Positive passion is magnetic and endlessly productive.

I'm passionate about passion just like I'm thoughtful about thought, or reflective about reflection.

The life of a philosopher might not be what you think. I clean the kitchen, load the dishes, and pick up in the yard after the dogs.

It's not all metaphysics all the time around here.

I have three female dogs who think they're dispossessed royalty and I'm their remaining retainer.

My dogs don't get the concept of "Pet" or "Pet Ownership." They seem to think they're using me for their own purposes.

Someone says I should talk to Cesar Milan!

Cesar Milan has had his effect here already, but unfortunately, on me! I'm "calm, submissive, philosophical."

I have rules, boundaries, and limitations.

Challenging times call for creativity and collaboration. Move forward innovatively! Move forward with partners!

A partner is an active collaborator, bringing his or her best to the joint endeavor each day.

Someone asked, in the light of Memorial Day, whether I would tweet on the concept of service. I'm glad to serve in this way!

When we honor service to the nation, it helps to reflect on what service is.

The English word, "service" comes to us ultimately from the Latin "servus" – an ancient word for slave.

It's ironic that the greatest form of human activity is named after the worst form of the human condition.

But life is shot through with paradox and irony. We often see the best somehow reflect and redeem the worst.

Service is concern and action for others.

Service puts others first. And, ironically, it's in acts of service that we most often feel our best and become our best.

Service lifts us up as we lift others up.

We never freely serve only someone else. True service to another always improves our own souls.

Service without love is a thin reflection of true service from the heart.

But any form of service can begin to mold our souls and expand us, if we allow it.

Business at its best is a form of service.

Family life at its best is a form of service.

Governmental work, at any level, should be a form of service.

Leadership in any context must be understood as service.

Patriotism, in the end, is about service: To our families, colleagues, neighbors, nation, and through our nation, to the world.

Take a moment to remember the service of others, and especially the forms that have involved the sacrifice of a life.

Whenever you see good service, use good words and give thanks.

Whenever you give good service, feel grateful for the chance.

One of our greatest freedoms is precisely our freedom to serve.

True service enlarges and inspires.

Service brings people together.

An act of genuine service taps into a need we have to meet a need others have. Service well done can fulfill us uniquely.

In the end, our lives will be evaluated not on how much money, power, fame, or status we have attained, but on how well we have served.

Someone has just mentioned those times in life when we feel like we don't fit in.

No one fits in everywhere. Finding where you fit is finding where you'll flourish!

Our emotional bruises are just the memorials of our efforts, and are like the degrees that the school of life confers on us.

The Stoics: Nothing has any power over my inner emotions and attitudes except that which I give it.

Nothing has any power over my soul's choice of virtue or vice except what I convey to it.

We can learn much from water, and the imagery it provides us.

When moving water encounters an obstacle, it goes around it, over it, or under it. Or it pushes it away. Be like water today.

What's stronger, water or stone? Stone is massive, dense, and hard. Dripping water can go right through it. Be like water today!

When things change enough, this liquid can become a solid. Change again? Steam. But it keeps its essence intact. Be like water today!

Water can be perfectly still, or come at us in waves. Be like water today!

Water calms. Water refreshes. Water excites. Water inspires. Be like water today!

Water can bubble up from the ground or come down from the sky. Be like water today!

Water flows on as it can and seeks its proper place. Be like water today!

When the world throws you a wrinkle, just steam it out! Be like water today!

Water you doing? Preserve your liquidity! Flow as you go! Be like water today!

Water gives life. And it's a necessity, not an option. Be like water today!

Like the fresh new dampness on the early morning grass, go dew something great! Be like water today!

Water attracts people to itself. They bring it their needs and their wants. Be like water today!

"The ocean is the greatest body of water, because it's lower than all the rest. They empty themselves into it." Hindu Proverb

True greatness arises from nobility and humility together!

Ha! Someone has just asked whether I was fish in a former life!

You're saying to yourself, "Eel write anything here, regardless of his porpoise!"

Just having fun, soaked through with imagery about water and life!

I'm overflowing with the metaphor of the moment!

This is part of what makes Twitter so great. When I look over the tweets of the last few minutes, I see Adult Swim at its best.

Well, friends, thanks! Enough of my fire hydrant of thoughts for the Twitter Stream right now! It's been nice to sit and think with you!

You guys are like a wisdom icemaker! Insights filtered through you are insights cubed!

I was just recognized as one of the top three retweeted people on Twitter! Amazing! Flooring! Amazing flooring here, nice oak.

I love it when a time of thinking together not only clarifies things for me, but resonates with others as well.

We should give ourselves one gift more often: conversation about things that matter with people we care about.

What can we do today to make life a little easier, happier, or exciting for someone else?

Remember at every moment: little things are noticed, and little things matter!

Your voice is your instrument. Use it beautifully today. You can bless or block another person with your tone.

You have a space. Draw others into it today. Share it well.

You have a purpose. Draw others into it today. Share it well.

You have a future. Draw others into it today. Share it well.

You have a gift. Bring it to others today. Watch it grow.

Any new thing faces the force of inertia! And that's just a test! Use greater power and overcome it!

Others around you have talents and gifts and purposes and missions. Find out how you can help! Serve them well and prosper!

Most of all: No matter what you do, or who you see today, pay attention with love.

There's nothing like a little early morning kitchen table Twitter philosophy!

I wish you Twisdom in all that you do!

A Note on the Text

The vast majority of these tweets are printed here as they initially appeared on Twitter, and in the same original sequence. But there have also been light edits to many. Several have been repositioned, for greater impact. And a few new transitional tweets have been added for greater flow here, to replace some of the live transitioning that happened in the context of their original spontaneous appearance on Twitter. They are all my individual contributions to the ongoing twitter conversation that is the cauldron of twisdom.

Some quotations are given in quote marks, and others are not, but all are attributed to the original sources, or at least to what seemed in the flurry of twitter-speed to be the original sources. We don't do footnotes on twitter. And what's the point of writing notes on your foot anyway? You can see them better if they're on your hand. I recommend ballpoint pen at the base of your thumb. I won't even get into endnotes. So if you want an original citation of historical sources alluded to here, use Google like I do when time allows, and may I wish you the best of good luck!

I have purposely avoided using almost all other Twitter names here – the many names of friends to whom some of these tweets originally were addressed, and who might have first asked me to reflect on one topic or another. I've done this to save the time and difficulty of tracking down who said what to whom, asking everyone to give me their email addresses, and then receive, sign, and return release forms by fax, mail, or scan, granting legal permission to use their names. This would have involved too much twitter work and too much time for the rapid publication that a project like this needs. The world is out there moving fast! We have to move with it! I'm sure that various Twitter friends may remember when they asked a question or made a comment that launched a particular stream of twisdom or spurred me to a particular tweet. I want to express my high regard and great affection for you all, which I'm about to do, in the next page of this book, the Acknowledgements! Keep goading me to think. I thank you for the thought.

Acknowledgments

I want to thank first all the great people who follow me on Twitter. You know who you are. If I tried to name you, one by one, I'd certainly leave someone out! You brighten my days, and help me to have an experience that no philosopher in human history has ever had. I hope that, in response, I sometimes manage to help you think something through in a new way, or tackle the new day with energy and enjoyment.

David Rendall and Ed Brenegar convinced me to try this new social medium, despite all my initial skepticism. To them, I owe all this subsequent fun and reflection. Mim Harrison, the Book and Publishing Guru at Levenger, and Levenger.com, offered her generous advice on the final form of the book. Dennis Walsak gave me the benefits of his expert design sensibilities and readied this for publication at world record speed.

I thank the founders of Twitter and their staff, and the staff at The Huffington Post, who have all given me very special places to extend my work as a contemporary philosopher.

I also want to thank two of my generous Twitter friends: Mariel Hemingway (MarielHemingway.com and .org) and Kathy Ireland (KathyIreland.com and .org), who did not think me forward to ask each of them to write a foreword for this fun little book. It's great to have an Oscar nominated actress and healthy living guru, along with an extraordinary entrepreneur and CEO who has also been one of the world's most famous models, both currently serving the globe through their respective businesses and brands, as Twitter partners in wisdom. May we continue our tweets together for a very long time!

I would like to invite you again, dear reader, if you haven't already done so, to join me at Twitter where I appear as TomVMorris. And please also join the people who are already in my circle of conversation there, where you'll find more great minds and hearts in one place than you ever could have imagined.

Tweet you later, cogitator!

Pooooof!!!!

Made in the USA
Lexington, KY
25 July 2013